Michael Leyton

Shape as Memory

A Geometric Theory of Architecture

Birkhäuser – Publishers for Architecture
Basel • Boston • Berlin

A CIP catalogue record for this book is available from the Library of Congress, Washington D.C., USA.

Deutsche Bibliothek Cataloging-in-Publication Data

Bibliographic information published by Die Deutsche Bibliothek
Die Deutsche Bibliothek lists this publication in the Deutsche Nationalbibliografie; detailed bibliographic data is available on the Internet at <http://dnb.ddb.de>.

Part of Springer Science+Business Media Publishing Group.
Printed on acid-free paper produced from chlorine-free pulp. TCF ∞
Printed in Germany

ISBN-13: 978-3-7643-7690-1
ISBN-10: 3-7643-76902

9 8 7 6 5 4 3 2 1 http://www.birkhauser.ch

Contents

History

by Antonino Saggio

History, which we Italians are so interested in, and whose relation with design we have studied so intensely – just what relation does history have with computers?
This is an apparently absurd question, but Michael Leyton answers it in this book. Let's take things one step at a time.
As you know, the great Italian architectural historian Bruno Zevi has always vehemently defended two theses. The first is that history is at the center of architectural activity. Zevi's view of history was a "critical" vision that emphasized the moments of change, the capacity to work within crises to formulate new hypotheses. His history was "non-" encyclopedic, "non-" philological; it was a history of architecture formed by successive breaks, by "heresies." It was, therefore, both a "counter-history" and a "constant" history of modernity.
Zevi's second fundamental thesis was the construction of a series of *invariants* like the *elenco,* overhanging structures, four-dimensional compositions and more. The invariants represented a series of transcendental values which were implicitly open and dynamic in their essence, which opposed academic rules. Zevi abhorred the static nature of forms, symmetry, the golden rules of proportion, the schema of treaty, manual and positivist typologies.
Up until now, these two theses, the centrality of the "critical" idea of history and the "dynamic" invariants, have lacked a conclusive connection tying the one to the other.
This connection has finally been provided by Michael Leyton, who explains in an incontrovertible manner that symmetry simultaneously kills both history and form!
Leyton is a prolific author of scientific texts for publishers like MIT Press and Springer; he is also a musician, a painter and a designer. But above all, he is a scholar who has codified a new way of thinking in this book. This is a new formalism. And the adjective "new," when dealing with formalism, is not a word to be used lightly.
The basis of Leyton's formalism is revolutionarily procedural in its nature. Let's try to understand how. Normally, a CAD (a program of the vector family which is now a part of every architect's computer) works on the "results." A CAD uses a series of lines of

code to describe the geometric forms created on the screen; it describes geometry through formulas that are primarily based on two large geometric families: mesh triangulations – by which even a very complex form can be reduced to a series of triangles – and the *spline* family, which organizes forms through sequences of mathematical equations.
If the object that is to be described is simple, just a few lines of code are needed; a complex object will require a great number of lines of code.
The basic idea of Leyton's reasoning, which is presented in this book, is: let's change the way we do things! Instead of thinking about the results, describing them in a geometric manner, let's concentrate on the process.
In one of Leyton's standard examples, take a piece of paper and crumple it up. The ensuing form is complex and, naturally, can be described and reproduced (with an enormous number of lines of code). But instead, think about creating a formalism based on the idea of process. In this case, to reproduce the form, I must simply say which force is to be applied to the specific "action" of crumpling. I therefore begin with a piece of paper and then apply the "formalism" of the act of crumpling it up.
The rise of this procedural way of thinking has important implications. First of all, from a practical point of view. It is no coincidence that big companies like IBM are very interested in the theses that Leyton has formulated as the basis of new computer languages. But an impressive series of implications can also be had in the biological, medical, and physical sciences and, naturally, in architectural science as well. Leyton has also resolved other questions along the way, like the relation with *Gestalt*, finally explaining a few unresolved points.
Let's go back to the point that is so important to us architects, and which brings us back to the title of the book, *Shape as Memory*, and to Zevi's two theories. Imagine a face with wrinkles, imagine a car that has a scratch on its door: these grooves reveal a history. Then, imagine a car and a face without history, without those signs. This is the basis of this book. And its relevant thesis. Form is the result of history or, in other words, form is memory!
A key aspect of Leyton's system is this: symmetrical choices (static, typological, blocked) represent the negation of form, the idea

of a form "with no history." This perfect, absolute ideal, which of course can be, as it has been, a pursued and a pursuable ideal, denies the very essence of form. As Leyton says: *Form is history*: form is not just the conscious acceptance of crises, agitation, difficulties; form itself is history. History, through this new formalism, is rooted in the past, but above all, it is launched toward the future. Form becomes open to new actions, to new processes.

Those like me, who have been brought up on Bruno Zevi's theories, find this logical connection exciting because this book backs it up with concise reasoning that is analytically incontrovertible.

Michael Leyton's book opens a new, and perhaps difficult, way of dealing with the computer revolution. Michael, with the intuition of a genius, but also with the hard work of a scholar, tries a new pathway that cannot not be explored further.

http://www.citicord.uniroma1.it/saggio/

Chapter 1
Geometry and Memory

1.1 Introduction

In my published books and papers, I have developed *new foundations to geometry* that are directly opposed to the foundations to geometry that have existed from Euclid to modern physics, including Einstein. These new foundations imply an entire restructuring of science, the replacement of its separate systems of laws (e.g., in quantum mechanics, relativity, etc.) with a common system of inference rules that unfold the environment as a world of deep "forensic information." In addition, there is a radical alteration in our understanding of design, and in particular, architecture: *New foundations to geometry mean new foundations to architecture.*

In order to see this, we must first contrast the foundations of geometry, as they have existed for almost 3,000 years, with the entirely opposite foundations presented in my books. The following statement summarizes the basic difference. It is then followed by a more detailed explanation of this difference.

Geometry

> CONVENTIONAL FOUNDATIONS FOR GEOMETRY: The geometric part of an object is that aspect which cannot store information about past action. Thus, in the conventional foundations, geometry is taken to be the study of memorylessness.
>
> NEW FOUNDATIONS FOR GEOMETRY: The geometric part of an object is that aspect which stores information about past action. Thus, in the new foundations, geometry is taken to be equivalent to memory storage.

1.2 Conventional Geometry: Euclid to Einstein

Radical as Einstein's theory of relativity might seem to be, it in fact goes back to the simple notion of ***congruence*** that is basic to Euclid. Thus, to understand the foundations of modern physics (including quantum mechanics), we should first look at the notion of congruence. Fig. 1.1 shows two triangles. To test if they are congruent, one translates and rotates the upper triangle to try to make it coincident with the lower one. If exact coinci-

dence is possible, one says that they are congruent. This allows one to regard the triangles as essentially the same.
In contrast, in the theory of geometry which I have developed, the two triangles are different because they must have different histories. For example, to convert the upper one into the lower one, it is necessary to add a history of translation and rotation.
Let us return to the Euclidean view. Simple as the notion of congruence is, it has been a major component of geometry for nearly 3,000 years, and was generalized in the late 19th century by Felix Klein in what is probably the most famous single lecture in the entire history of mathematics – his inaugural lecture at Erlangen. In this lecture, Klein defined a program, which is the most frequently cited foundation for geometry:

> KLEIN'S ERLANGEN PROGRAM
> A geometric object is an invariant under some chosen system of transformations.

This statement can be illustrated in the following way: Consider the upper triangle in Fig. 1.1. It has a number of properties: (1) It has three sides, (2) it points upward, (3) it has two equal angles, and so on. Now apply a movement to make it coincident with the lower triangle. Properties (1) and (3) remain invariant (unchanged); i.e., the lower triangle has three sides and has two equal angles. In contrast, property (2) is not invariant, i.e., the triangle no longer points upwards. Klein said that the geometric properties are those that remain invariant; i.e., properties (1) and

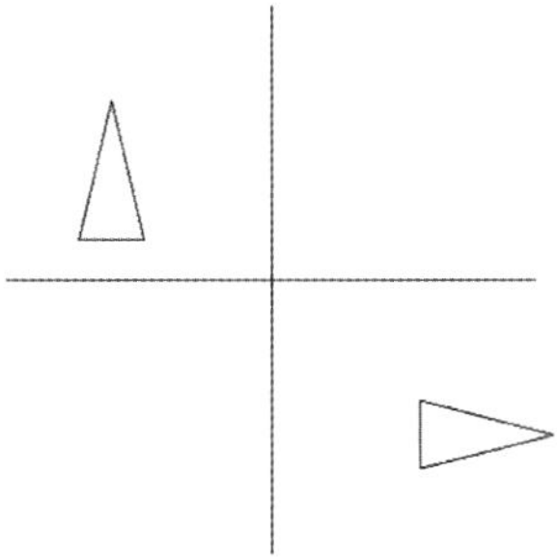

Figure 1.1: Establishing congruence

(3). Most crucially for our concern: *Because these properties are unchanged (invariant) under the movement, it is impossible to infer from them that the movement has taken place. Only the non-invariant property, the direction of pointing, allows us to recover the movement.* In the terminology of my geometric research, I therefore argue this:

> KLEIN'S PROGRAM CONCERNS MEMORYLESSNESS
> Past actions cannot be inferred from features that are unchanged under those actions, i.e., from invariants. Therefore, invariants cannot act as memory stores. Thus, Klein views geometry as the study of memorylessness.

Klein's approach became the basis of 20th-century mathematics and physics. As an example, let us turn to Special and General Relativity.

1.3 Special and General Relativity

The significance of Einstein's theory of relativity is that it is the first theory in physics that was founded on Klein's program for geometry. Since then, all the other branches of physics, such as quantum mechanics and quantum field theory, have been based on Klein's program. Let us now show the relationship between Einstein's work and Klein's. Einstein's theory of relativity is founded on the following principle:

> EINSTEIN'S PRINCIPLE OF RELATIVITY
> The proper objects of physics are those that are invariant (unchanged) under changes of reference frame.

To illustrate this principle, consider Fig. 1.2. Each of the planes represents the reference frame of a different observer. Let us suppose that each observer measures the length of the same *interval in space* (i.e., between two known points such as the ends of a building). Because the observers are in different reference frames, they find that the length is different in their different frames. Therefore according to Einstein's Principle of Relativity (above), length is not a proper object of physics – because it is not an invariant under changes of reference frame. However, if one takes a *space-time* interval, rather than just a space interval,

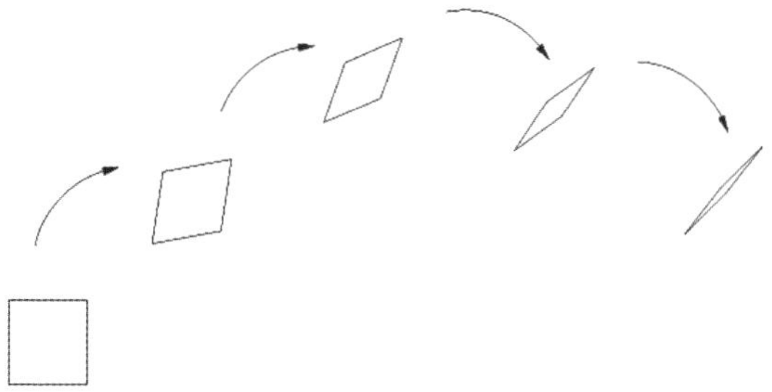

Figure 1.2: Transformations between reference frames.

this turns out to have the same length in the different frames; i.e., it is an invariant under changes of reference frame. Thus, according to Einstein's Principle of Relativity (above), space-time intervals are proper objects of physics.

Notice that Fig. 1.2 also shows the transformations (arrows) that go between the reference frames, i.e., that change the frames into each other. Einstein's Principle of Relativity says that the proper objects of physics are those that are invariant under the *transformations* that change one frame into another. For example, a space-time interval is an invariant (unchanged) under the *transformations* that go between reference frames.

It is important now to see that this is an example of Klein's theory of geometry. Recall from section 1.2 that Klein said that a geometric object is an invariant under some chosen system of transformations. In relativity, the chosen transformations are those that go between the reference frames of different observers. Since Klein says that a *geometric object* is an invariant under the chosen transformations, Einstein's Principle of Relativity says that a space-time interval is a *geometric object*; i.e., an invariant under the transformations between reference frames. Generally, therefore, Einstein's Principle of Relativity says that the proper objects of physics are the *geometric objects* (invariants) of the transformations between reference frames. Thus Einstein is credited with what is called the *geometrization* of physics.

In Special Relativity, the chosen transformations (between reference frames) are called the Lorentz transformations. In General Relativity, the chosen transformations are more general – they are arbitrary deformations. Therefore we say:

Einstein's Geometrization of Physics

The proper objects of physics are the geometric objects (invariants) under changes of reference frame. In Special Relativity, these are the geometric objects (invariants) of the Lorentz transformations. In General Relativity, these are the geometric objects (invariants) of arbitrary deformations.

Now recall from section 1.2 that Klein's invariants program concerns memorylessness.
This is because past action cannot be inferred from an invariant.
Thus, I argue the following:

Einstein is anti-memory

Since Einstein's Theory of Relativity is aimed at the extraction of invariants, it concerns memorylessness.

The same situation exists in Quantum Mechanics. For example, the modern classification of particles was invented by Eugene Wigner, and is carried out by the extraction of invariants of measurement operators. We can therefore say that the two cornerstones of modern physics – Relativity and Quantum Mechanics – are founded on memorylessness.
It is important now to observe that Klein's invariants program really originates with Euclid's notion of congruence: Invariants are those properties that allow congruence. Therefore, the congruent properties are those that have no history. In conclusion, I argue the following:

Memorylessness from Euclid to Modern Physics

The basis of modern physics can be traced back to Euclid's concern with congruence. We can therefore say that the entire history of geometry, from Euclid to modern physics, has been founded on the notion of memorylessness.

1.4 New Foundations to Geometry

The previous sections have described the conventional foundations of geometry. We now turn to the entirely opposite foundations which have been elaborated in my books. In particular, the conceptual foundations were presented in my book *Symmetry, Causality, Mind* (MIT Press, 630 pages); and the full mathemati-

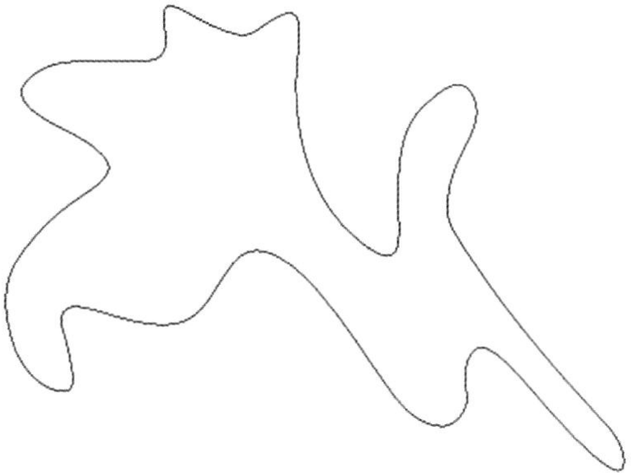

Figure 1.3: Shape as history

cal theory was presented in my book *A Generative Theory of Shape* (Springer-Verlag, 550 pages). Let us understand the fundamental difference between the conventional foundations and new foundations.

As we have seen, the conventional foundations state that the proper objects of geometry are invariants, i.e., those features that do not retain past history. In contrast, my new foundations state that geometry should really be the study of those features that retain information about the past; i.e., geometry is the study of memory. We will now begin to understand these new foundations. Consider the shape in Fig. 1.3. One clearly sees it as the consequence of various deforming actions – protrusion, indentation, squashing, resistance. These actions occurred in the past, and yet, somehow, one is able to infer this history from the shape itself. The claim I am making is this:

Shape is the means of reconstructing history.

In relation to this, let us return to the important term, *memory*. An object from which one can recover information about the past is generally called a *memory store*. Therefore, what is being proposed here is this:

Shape is the means by which past actions are stored.

In fact, according to my new foundations for geometry, shape and memory storage are equivalent. In other words:

Shape = Memory Storage

I will later propose the basic rules by which memory is stored in shape. But first it is necessary to clearly understand that part of a shape in which memory cannot be stored. For this, return to Fig. 1.1 which shows the two triangles. We noted that the upper triangle has a number of properties: (1) three sides, (2) points upward, (3) two equal angles. We saw that, after applying the translation and rotation to make it coincident with the lower triangle, properties (1) and (3) remain invariant (unchanged); i.e., the lower triangle has three sides and has two equal angles.
Most crucially, because these properties are unchanged (invariant) under the movement, it is impossible to infer from them that the movement has taken place. Therefore, we are led to the following fundamental conclusion:

Invariants cannot act as memory stores.

Only non-invariant properties can act as memory stores.
The inverse relation between invariance and memory storage can be illustrated by considering the shape of the human body. One can recover, from the shape, the history of embryological development and subsequent growth, that the body underwent. The shape is full of its history. Simultaneously, one should observe the following: There is very little that is *congruent* between the developed body and the original spherical egg from which it arose. There is very little that has remained *invariant* from the origin state. The new foundations of geometry state that the shape, e.g., of the human body, is equivalent to the history that can be recovered from it. Furthermore, I argue that this view of geometry is the appropriate one for the computational age. A computational system is founded on the use of memory stores. Our age is concerned with the retention of memory rather than the loss of it. We try to buy computers with greater memory, not less. People are worried about declining into old age, because memory decreases. Intelligence is dependent on memory.
Now let us turn to architecture. What I am going to argue is this:

FOUNDATIONS FOR ARCHITECTURE
Conventional foundations: *There is a correspondence between geometry of the last 3,000 years and architecture of the last 3,000 years. Both are concerned with maximizing memorylessness.*
New foundations: *There is a correspondence between the new foundations for geometry, developed in my previous books, and the new foundations for architecture, developed in the present book. These foundations are concerned with maximizing memory storage.*

1.5 The Memory Roles of Symmetry and Asymmetry

The fundamental proposals will now be given for the new theory of geometry, and this will lead to a new approach to architecture. Since the architectural theory is based on maximizing memory storage, it is necessary to answer the following question: How can an object become a memory store, i.e., a source of information about the past? Before we can understand this, let us first understand what form memory stores can take.

According to the new foundations for geometry, every feature of the world is a memory store. Let us consider some examples. A *scar* on a person's face is, in fact, a memory store. It gives us information about the past: It tells us that, in the past, the surface of the skin was cut. A *dent* in a car door is also a memory store; i.e., information about the past can be extracted from this. The dent tells us that, in the past, there was an impact on the car. Any *growth* is a memory store. For example, the shape of a person's face gives us information of the past history of growth that occurred; e.g., the nose and cheekbones grew outward, the wrinkles folded in, etc. Similarly, the shape of a tree gives us information about how it grew. Therefore, from both a face and a tree, we can retrieve information about the past. A *scratch* on a piece of furniture is a memory store, because we can extract from it information that, in the past, the surface had contact with a sharp moving object. A *crack* in a vase is a memory store because it informs us that, in the past, the vase underwent some impact; i.e., this information is retrievable from the crack.

I argue that the world is, in fact, simply layers and layers of memory storage (information about the past). One can illustrate this by looking at the relationships between the examples just listed. For instance, consider a scar on a person's face. First, the scar is information about the past scratching. However, this is on a per-

son's face which is information about past growth. Thus the scar is a memory store that sits on the face which is a memory store. As another example consider a crack on a vase. The crack stores the information about the past hitting. However, this sits on a vase which stores the information about how the vase was formed from clay on the potter's wheel. For example, the vertical height of the vase is information about the past process that pushed the clay upwards; and the outline of the vase, curving in and out, is information of the past changing pressure that occurred in the potter's hands. Therefore, the crack is a memory store of hitting which sits on the vase which is a memory store of clay-manipulation.
We have seen that, on a concrete level, memory stores can take an enormous variety of forms – e.g., scars, dents, growths, scratches, cracks, etc. In fact, there are probably infinitely many types of memory stores. However, I argue that, on an abstract level, all stores have only one form:

Memory is stored in Asymmetries.

Correspondingly:

Memory is erased by Symmetries.

These two principles will be illustrated many times in this book; but let us begin with a simple example: Consider the sheet of paper shown on the left in Fig. 1.4. Even if one had never seen that sheet before, one would conclude that it had undergone the action of twisting. The reason is that the asymmetry in the

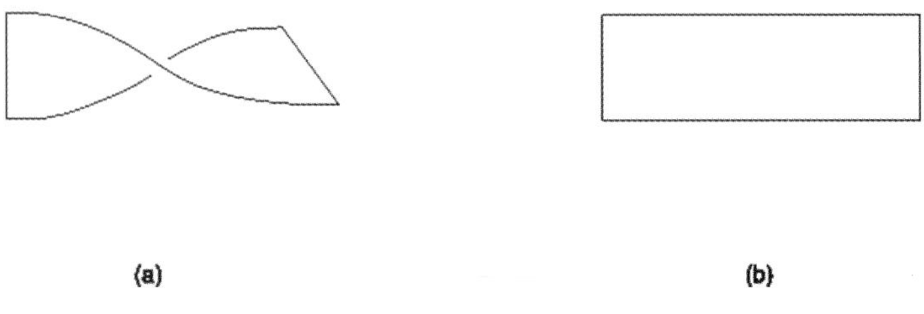

Figure 1.4: A twisted sheet is a source of information about the past. A non-twisted sheet is not.

sheet allows one to retrieve the past history. Thus, the asymmetry is acting as a memory store.
Now let us un-twist the paper, thus obtaining the straight sheet shown on the right in Fig. 1.4. Suppose we show this straight sheet to any person on the street. They would *not* be able to infer from it that it had once been twisted. The reason is that the symmetry of the straight sheet has wiped out the ability to recover the past history. That is, *the symmetry has erased the memory store*. Notice that there is a feature associated with the fact that the symmetry erases the memory store: From the symmetry, the inference is that the straight sheet had always been like this. For example, when you take a sheet from a box of paper you have just bought, you do not assume that it had once been twisted or crumpled. Its very straightness (symmetry) leads you to conclude that it had always been straight.
The two above statements – one about asymmetries and the other about symmetries – will now be formulated as the following two inference rules.

> ASYMMETRY PRINCIPLE
> An asymmetry in the present is understood as having originated from a past symmetry.
> SYMMETRY PRINCIPLE
> A symmetry in the present is understood as having always existed.

At first, it might seem as if there are many exceptions to these two rules. In fact, all the apparent exceptions are due to incorrect descriptions of situations. These rules cannot be violated for logical reasons, as was shown in my previous books.
Now some important observations should be made: First, it is crucial to understand that the Asymmetry and Symmetry Principles are *inference rules*. Thus memory storage is viewed here as a process of inference. In fact, we have this:

> MEMORY RETRIEVAL AS FORENSIC INFERENCE
> The following theory of memory retrieval is being proposed here:
> Memory retrieval is the application of a set of inference rules to an object such that the rules extract information about past actions applied to the object. Thus, memory retrieval is viewed as a process of forensic inference.

This also leads to the following:

FORENSIC THEORY OF GEOMETRY
Whereas the conventional theory of geometry is founded on descriptive axioms (e.g., statements such as "two distinct points lie on exactly one line"), my theory of geometry is founded on *inference rules*. In fact, since these inference rules are forensic, my theory can be regarded as a forensic theory of geometry.

1.6 Basic Procedure for Recovering the Past

I will now argue that the recovery of the past can be carried out by the following simple procedure:

PROCEDURE FOR RECOVERING THE PAST
(1) Partition the presented situation into its asymmetries and symmetries.
(2) Apply the Asymmetry Principle to the asymmetries.
(3) Apply the Symmetry Principle to the symmetries.

An extended example will now be considered that will illustrate the power of this procedure, as follows: In a set of psychological experiments that I carried out in 1982 in the psychology department in Berkeley, I found that when subjects are presented with a rotated parallelogram, as shown in Fig. 1.5a, their minds go through the sequence of shapes shown in Fig. 1.5. It is important to understand that the subjects are presented with only the first shape. The rest of the shapes are actually generated by their own minds, as a response to the presented shape.

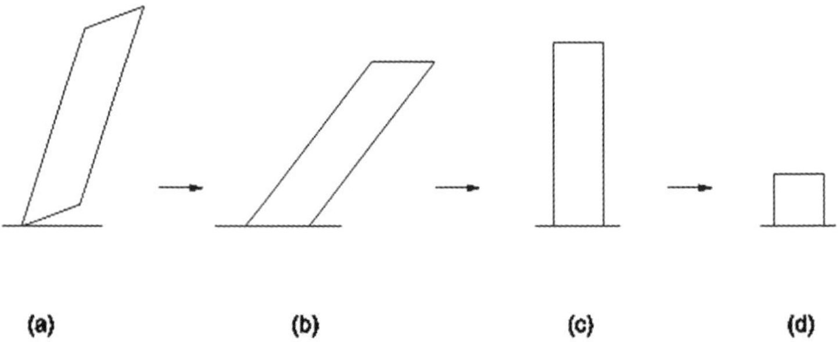

Figure 1.5: The history inferred from a rotated parallelogram.

Examination of the results indicates that what the subjects are doing is explaining how the first shape (Fig. 1.5a) was created. In other words, they are saying that, in the previous stage, the rotated parallelogram was non-rotated (Fig. 1.5b); and in the stage before that, it was a rectangle (Fig. 1.5c); and in the stage before that, it was a square (Fig. 1.5d).
Notice that this means that the sequence shown in Fig. 1.5 represents the *reversal of time* from the rotated parallelogram. This, and many examples in my research, lead me to the following conclusion:

The mind runs time backwards from objects.

We shall now see that the method by which the subjects create this sequence is by using the Asymmetry Principle and the Symmetry Principle, i.e., the two above laws for the reconstruction of history. Recall that the way one uses the two laws is to apply our simple three-stage Procedure for Recovering the Past, given above: (1) Partition the presented situation into its asymmetries and symmetries, (2) apply the Asymmetry Principle to the asymmetries, and (3) apply the Symmetry Principle to the symmetries.
Thus, to use this procedure on the rotated parallelogram, let us begin by identifying the asymmetries in that figure. First, it is important to note that the most fundamental definition of asymmetries (in both mathematics and physics) is this: Asymmetries are *distinguishabilities*; i.e., differences.
Now, in the rotated parallelogram, there are three distinguishabilities (differences):

(1) The distinguishability between the orientation of the shape and the orientation of the environment – indicated by the difference between the bottom edge of the shape and the horizontal line which it touches.
(2) The distinguishability between adjacent angles in the shape: they are different sizes.
(3) The distinguishability between adjacent sides in the shape: they are different lengths.

Therefore, examining the sequence, from the rotated parallelogram to the square, we see that these three distinguishabilities are removed successively backwards in time, as follows: (1) The removal of the first distinguishability, that between the orientation of the shape and the orientation of the environment, results in the transition from the rotated parallelogram to the non-rotated one. (2) The removal of the second distinguishability, that between adjacent angles, results in the transition from the non-rotated parallelogram to the rectangle, where the angles are equalized. (3) The removal of the third distinguishability, that between adjacent sides, results in the transition from the rectangle to the square, where the sides are equalized.

The conclusion is therefore this: *Each successive step in the sequence is a use of the Asymmetry Principle, which says that an asymmetry must be returned to a symmetry backwards in time.*

We have just identified the asymmetries in the rotated parallelogram, and applied the Asymmetry Principle to each of these. We now identify the symmetries in the rotated parallelogram and apply the Symmetry Principle to each of these. First, it is important to note that the most fundamental definition of symmetries (in both mathematics and physics) is this: Symmetries are *indistinguishabilities*; i.e., equalities.

In the rotated parallelogram, there are two indistinguishabilities (equalities):

(1) The opposite angles are indistinguishable in size.
(2) The opposite sides are indistinguishable in size.

Now, the Symmetry Principle requires that these two symmetries in the rotated parallelogram must be preserved backwards in time. And indeed, this turns out to be the case. Thus, the first symmetry, the equality between opposite angles, in the rotated parallelogram, is preserved backwards through the sequence. That is, each subsequent shape, from left to right, has the property that opposite angles are equal. Similarly, the other symmetry, the equality between opposite sides in the rotated parallelogram, is preserved backwards through the sequence. That is, each subsequent shape, from left to right, has the property that opposite sides are equal.

Thus, to summarize the full example: The sequence from the rotated parallelogram to the square is determined by two rules: the Asymmetry Principle which returns asymmetries to symmetries, and the Symmetry Principle which preserves the symme-

Figure 1.6: An administration building conforming to the conventional foundations for geometry.

Figure 1.7: The first Administration Building.

tries. These two rules allow us to recover the history, i.e., run time backwards.

1.7 Architecture

I argue this: *The conventional foundations for geometry correspond to the conventional foundations for architecture. The new foundations for geometry correspond to new foundations for architecture.*

Let us examine this in more detail. We saw in section 1.2 that the conventional foundations of geometry, which have existed for almost 3,000 years, are based on congruence and its generalization as invariance. Indeed, in these foundations, a *geometric object* is defined as an invariant.

Invariance is closely related to *symmetry* in the following way: In mathematics, one says that an object is symmetric if it is indistinguishable from transformed versions of itself; e.g., an object is reflectionally symmetric if it is indistinguishable from its reflected versions, or an object is rotationally symmetric if it is indistinguishable from its rotated versions. Therefore an object is *symmetric* if it is *invariant* under certain transformations. This has been the basis of the conventional foundations of geometry. For example, in Einstein's theory, the system of transformations that act between reference frames, and produce the invariants of relativity theory, necessarily act symmetrically on space-time. Generally, therefore, a geometry based on maximizing invariants is based on maximizing symmetry.

However, one of my basic principles says that memory (information about the past) is not extractable from a symmetry; in fact, symmetry erases memory storage. Therefore, conventional geometry is based on maximizing memorylessness.

In relation to this, consider architecture. It is clear that the conventional foundations of geometry produced the type of buildings that have been seen since the beginning of architecture. Whether one considers the Greek temple, the Gothic cathedral, the Renaissance palace, the French chateau, the 19th-century bank, the 20th-century skyscraper, each is governed by symmetry. Each, therefore, concerns the erasure of memory.

In contrast, consider my new foundations for geometry. Rather than defining the geometric object as the memoryless object (the invariant), as in the conventional foundations, the new foundations define the geometric object as the opposite: the memory store. In fact, according to my new foundations, shape is equivalent to memory storage. In particular, the claim is that all memory storage takes place via shape. The goal of these new foundations is to set up a system of rules that *maximize* memory storage. These rules are inference rules for the recovery of process-history. The fundamental rule is that memory is stored only in *asymmetries*.

This gives an entirely new basis for architecture: *Whereas conventional architecture is based on symmetry – and therefore erasure of memory – the new architecture is based on asymmetry – and therefore the storage of memory*.

The goal of my architectural theory and practice, therefore, becomes the elaboration of means by which memory can be stored in the structure of a building. This book develops the mathematical principles by which this is possible. My designs for *The Administration Building* illustrate the use of these principles to create a new type of building.

This section ends with photographs of the two opposite kinds of buildings. First, Fig. 1.6 shows a conventional type of adminstration building – i.e., based on the conventional foundations of geometry. It is a symmetrical structure. It stores nothing. It is impervious to the vicissitudes of time. It stands aloof, disinterested, dull, and institutional.

In contrast, Fig. 1.7 shows one of my own administration buildings. This alive structure is highly asymmetric and therefore allows us to recover the history of the diverse processes that produced it – bending, cutting, twisting, breaking, grappling, bludgeoning, etc. It is, therefore, the store of a past history. It is no longer dull and aloof, like the conventional building. It is alive with time, and, because it is filled with memory, it is alive with mind.

Chapter 2
A Process-Grammar for Shape

2.1 Curvature as Memory Storage

The purpose of this chapter is to illustrate the principles of the previous chapter, by showing that a large amount of memory can be stored in a particular type of asymmetry: the *curvature extrema* of a shape. Thus, if the architect uses curvature extrema, he or she can significantly increase the history stored in a building.

First let us understand clearly what a curvature extremum is. For curves in the plane, the term *curvature* can be regarded simply as the amount of bend. Fig. 2.1 illustrates this. The line at the top has no bend and thus has zero curvature. As one moves down the series of lines, the amount of bend (curvature) increases.

An important feature about the bottom line in Fig. 2.1 should now be observed. It has a special point E where the curvature is greater than at any other point on the line. For example, notice that at points G and H the curve is actually flatter. Thus one says that E is a *curvature extremum*.

According to Chapter 1, memory is constructed by the use of *inference rules*; i.e., this is a forensic theory of geometry. Thus, I will show that curvature extrema are powerful information sources for the *inference* of the past history of an object. To do this, I will be applying the two fundamental inference rules introduced in section 1.5: the Asymmetry Principle and Symmetry Principle. For illustration purposes, the discussion will be confined to smooth closed curves in the 2D plane. Such curves can represent the outlines of many biological shapes, e.g., amoebas, embryos, biological organs, human beings, etc., as well as non-living entities such as spilt coffee, rain puddles, etc. My mathe-

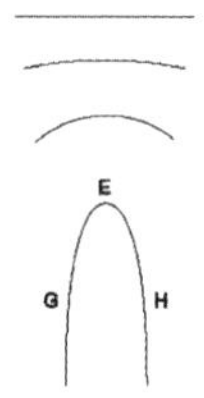

Figure 2.1: Successively increasing curvature.

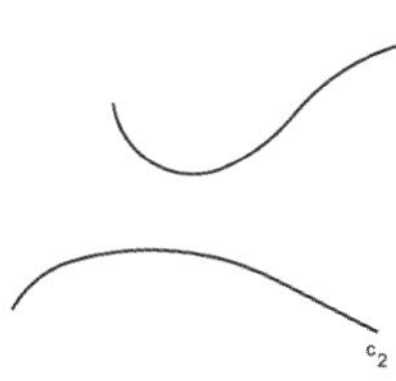

Figure 2.2: How can one construct a symmetry axis between these two curves?

matical research shows that it is easy to extend the argument to non-smooth shapes, and to 3D shapes.

2.2 General Symmetry Axes

It is first necessary to understand how symmetry can be defined in complex shape. Clearly, in a simple shape, such as an equilateral triangle, a symmetry axis is easy to define. One simply places a straight mirror across the shape such that one half is reflected onto the other. The straight line of the mirror is then defined to be a symmetry axis of the shape. However, in a complex shape, it is often impossible to place a mirror that will reflect one half of the figure onto the other. Fig. 1.3 on page 13 is an example of such a shape. However, in such cases, one might still wish to regard the figure, or part of it, as symmetrical about some *curved* axis. Such a generalized axis can be constructed in the following way.

Consider Fig. 2.2. It shows two curves c_1 and c_2, which can be understood as two sides of an object. Notice that no mirror could reflect one of these curves onto the other. The goal is to construct a symmetry axis between the two curves. One proceeds as follows: As shown in Fig. 2.3, introduce a circle that is tangential simultaneously to the two curves. Here the two tangent points are marked as A and B.

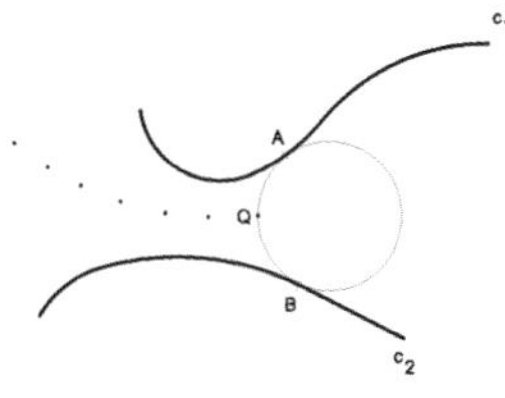

Figure 2.3: The points Q define the simmetry axis.

Next, move the circle continuously along the two curves, c_1 and c_2, while always ensuring that it maintains the property of being tangential to the two curves simultaneously. To maintain this double-touching property, it might be necessary to expand or contract the circle. Finally, on any circle, mark the point shown as Q in Fig. 2.3. This is the point on the circle, half-way between the two tangent points. As the circle moves along the curves, the points Q trace out a trajectory, as indicated by the sequence of dots shown in the figure. I define this to be the *symmetry axis* of the two curves.

2.3 Symmetry-Curvature Duality

Recall that the goal of this chapter is to show that curvature extrema can act as powerful memory stores; i.e., valuable historical information can be inferred from them. However, our rules for the extraction of memory depend on the phenomenon of *symmetry*. This means that we must find a connection between symmetry and curvature.

In fact, forming such a connection presents a problem that is deep in the foundations of mathematics. There are two main branches of mathematics: algebra and topology. Algebra is the study of structures of combination; whereas topology is the study of neighborhood structures. Reflectional symmetry belongs to the first branch, and curvature belongs to the second. Thus, on shape, symmetry is constructed across regions, whereas curvature is measured within a region. Reflectional symmetry is a discrete property, whereas curvature is a smooth property.

Despite the fact that there is a fundamental difference between symmetry and curvature, a deep link was shown between the two in a theorem that I proposed and proved in the journal *Computer Vision, Graphics, Image Processing*. This theorem will be a crucial step in our argument:

> SYMMETRY-CURVATURE DUALITY THEOREM (LEYTON, 1987):
> Any section of curve, that has one and only one curvature extremum, has one and only one symmetry axis. This axis is forced to terminate at the extremum itself.

The theorem can be illustrated by looking at Fig. 2.4. On the curve shown, there are three extrema: m1, M, m2. Therefore, on

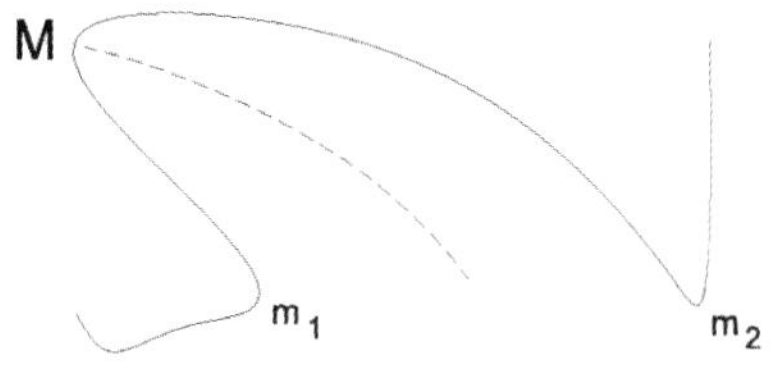

Figure 2.4: Illustration of the Symmetry-Curvature Duality Theorem.

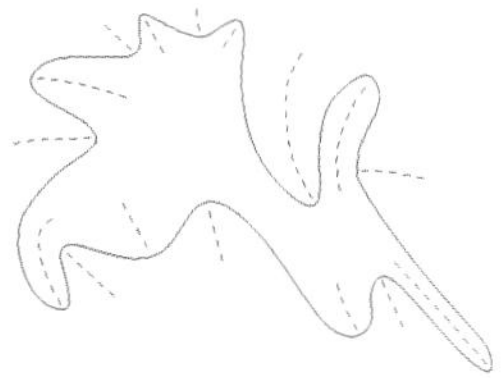

Figure 2.5: Sixteen extrema imply sixteen symmetry axes.

the section of curve *between* extrema m1 and m2, there is only one extremum, M. What the theorem says is this: Because this section of curve has only one extremum, it has only one symmetry axis. This axis is forced to terminate at the extremum M. The axis is shown as the dashed line in the figure.

It is valuable to illustrate the theorem on a closed shape, for example, that shown in Fig. 2.5. This shape has sixteen curvature extrema. Therefore, the above theorem tells us that there are sixteen unique symmetry axes associated with, and terminating at, the extrema. They are given as the dashed lines shown in the figure.

2.4 The Interaction Principle

With the Symmetry-Curvature Duality Theorem, it now becomes possible to use our two fundamental principles for the extraction of history from shape: the Asymmetry Principle and the Symmetry Principle. In this section, we use the Symmetry Principle, and in the next, we use the Asymmetry Principle.

The Symmetry Principle says that a symmetry in the present is preserved backwards in time. Notice that this means that symmetry axes must be preserved backwards in time. In my previous research, I have shown that this occurs if the processes run along the axes. The result is the following rule, which has been corroborated extensively in both shape and motion perception:

> INTERACTION PRINCIPLE (LEYTON, 1984):
> Symmetry axes are the directions along which processes are hypothesized as most likely to have acted.

2.5 Undoing Curvature Variation

Although the Interaction Principle tells us that the processes must have acted along the symmetry axes, it does not tell us what the processes actually did to the shape. For that, we must use the Asymmetry Principle, which states that, in running time backward, asymmetry is removed. In the present case, the asymmetry to be considered will be *distinguishability in curvature*; i.e., differences in curvature (bend) around the curve. Therefore, differences in curvature must be removed backwards in time. Observe that this means that one eventually arrives back at a circle, because the circle is the only smooth closed curve without curvature distinguishability; i.e. every point on a circle has the same curvature as every other point. To conclude: The Asymmetry Principle implies *that the ultimate past of any smooth closed curve must have been a circle*.

With respect to this, consider again the Interaction Principle, which says that the past processes moved along the symmetry axes evident in the present shape. Incorporating this now with the use of the Asymmetry Principle, we conclude that the past processes moved along the axes pushing the boundary to create the distinguishabilities in curvature. For instance: Each protrusion in Fig. 2.5 was the result of *pushing the boundary out* along its

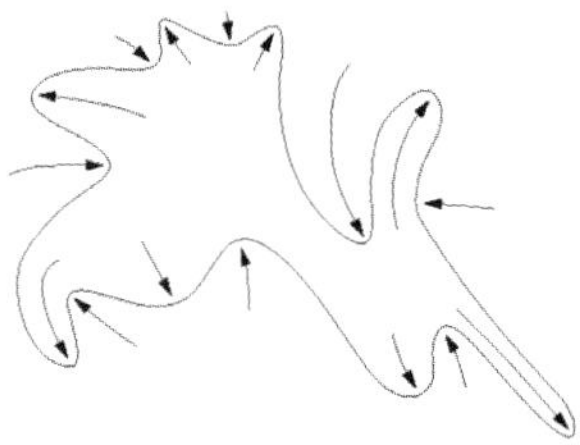

Figure 2.6: The processes inferred by the rules.

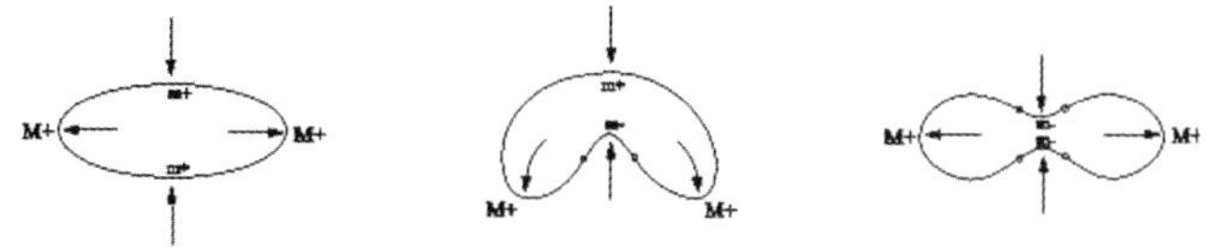

Figure 2.7: The inferred histories on the shapes with 4 extrema.

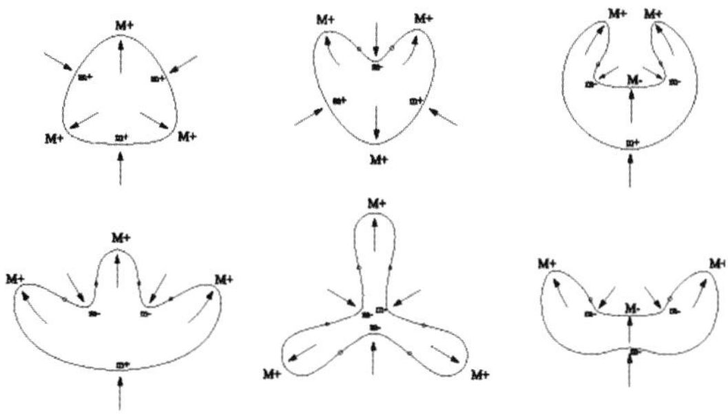

Figure 2.8: The inferred histories on the shapes with 6 extrema.

associated axis, and each indentation was the result of *pushing the boundary in* along its axis. One therefore sees that each axis is the *trace* or *record* of boundary-movement. Taking the earlier shape, Fig. 2.5, one now understands the axes as *arrows*, along which the processes went, as shown in Fig. 2.6.
In particular, one can now understand the significance of the curvature extrema. These are the end-points of the processes as they moved along the traces. In fact, one can consider the traces to be those of the curvature extrema as they were being pushed along the axes.

2.6 Extensive Application

So far, in this chapter, we have developed three rules for the extraction of history from curvature extrema. They are:

RULE 1. The Symmetry-Curvature Duality Theorem: This says that each curvature extremum has a unique axis leading to, and terminating at, the extremum.
RULE 2. A particular version of the Symmetry Principle, called the Interaction Principle: This says that the processes, which created the shape, went along symmetry axes.
RULE 3. A particular use of the Asymmetry Principle: This use says that differences in curvature must be removed backwards in time.

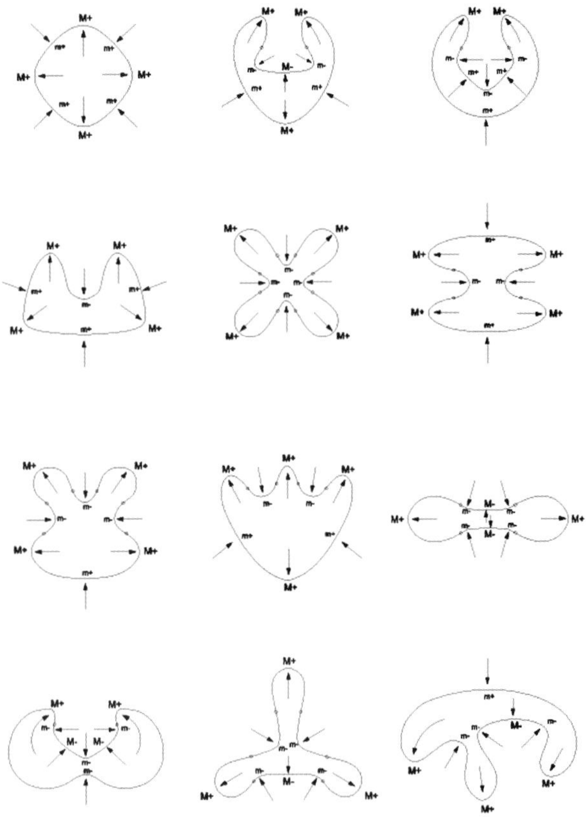

Figure 2.9: The inferred histories on the shapes with 8 extrema.

To obtain extensive corroboration for the above rules, let us now apply them to all shapes with up to eight curvature extrema. These are shown as the outlines in Figs. 2.7-2.9. When our inference rules are applied to these outlines, they produce the arrows shown as the inferred histories. One can see that the results accord remarkably well with intuition.

Further considerations should be made: Any individual outline, together with the inferred arrows, will be called a *process diagram*. The reader should observe that on each process diagram in Figs. 2.7-2.9, a letter-label has been placed at each extremum (the end of each arrow). There are four alternative labels, M^+, m^-, m^+, and M^-, and these correspond to the four alternative types of curvature extrema. The four types are shown in Fig. 2.10 and are explained as follows:

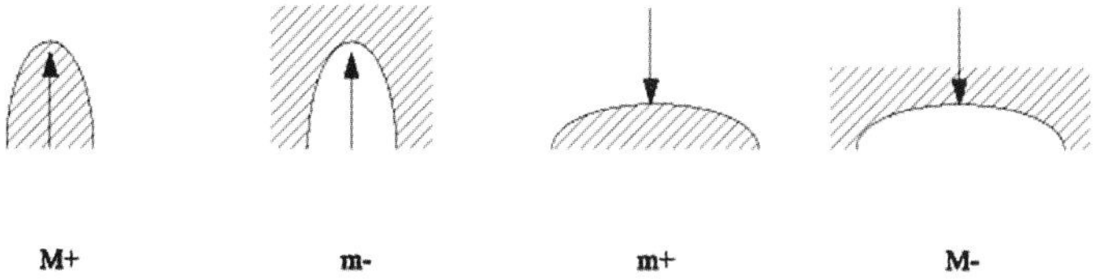

Figure 2.10: The four types of extrema.

The first two have exactly the same shape: They are the sharpest kinds of curvature extrema. The difference between them is that, in the first, the solid (shaded) is on the inside, and, in the second, the solid (shaded) is on the outside. That is, they are figure/ground reversals of each other. The remaining two extrema are also figure/ground reversals of each other. Here the extrema are the flattest points on the respective curves.

Now notice the following important phenomenon: In surveying the shapes in Figs. 2.7-2.9, it becomes clear that the four extrema types correspond to four English terms that people use to describe *processes*:

Extremum Type	↔	Process Type
M^+	↔	protrusion
m^-	↔	indentation
m^+	↔	squashing
M^-	↔	resistance

2.7 A Grammatical Decomposition of the Asymmetry Principle

The third of the three curvature rules proposed above was a particular example of the Asymmetry Principle. What we will now do is decompose this rule into components that yield additional information concerning the past history of the shape.

To understand this approach, let us imagine that we have two stages in the history of the shape. For example, imagine yourself to be a doctor looking at two X-rays of a tumor taken a month apart. Observe that any doctor examines two such X-rays (e.g., on a screen), in order to assess what has happened in the intervening month. This is exactly the type of problem we will solve now.

Problem: What is the deformational history that bridges any two stages in the evolution of a shape?

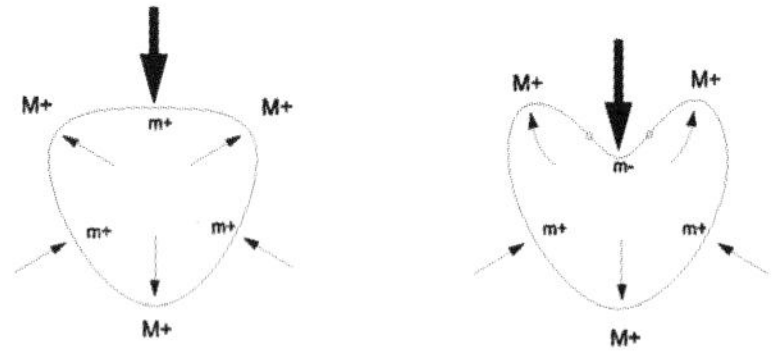

Figure 2.11: The downward squashing arrow (left shape) continues till it indents (right shape).

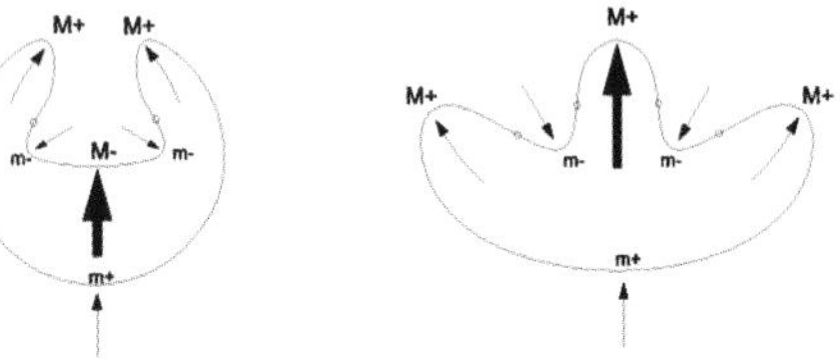

Figure 2.12: The upward resistance arrow (left shape) continues till it protrudes (right shape).

Solution: In a paper I published in 1988, I showed that mathematically, the deformational history can be composed of only six types of events at curvature extrema; i.e., these six types constitute a grammar that can construct any deformational history. I called this the *Process-Grammar*. Although the six types of events were defined mathematically, they are very easy to describe intuitively, thus:

1. SQUASHING CONTINUES TILL IT INDENTS: This is illustrated in Fig. 2.11. Observe that the downward squashing arrow in the left shape explains the flattening that exists at the top of that shape relative to the sharpening that exists toward the sides of the shape. In this situation, the squashing arrow continues to push and eventually indents, as shown in the right shape.

2. RESISTANCE CONTINUES TILL IT PROTRUDES: This is illustrated in Fig. 2.12. We are considering the upward bold arrow in the left shape. The process at this extremum is an *internal resistance*. In order to understand this process, let us suppose that the left shape represents an island. Initially, this island was circular. Then, there was an inflow of water at the top (creating a dip inwards). This flow increased inward, but met a ridge of mountains along

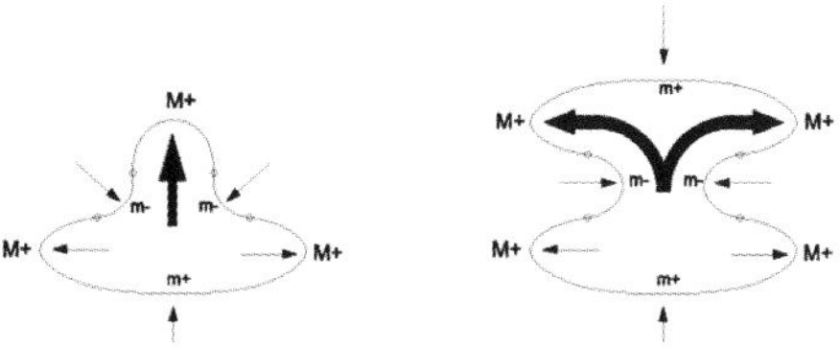

Figure 2.13: The upward arrow (left shape) branches to form a shield (right shape).

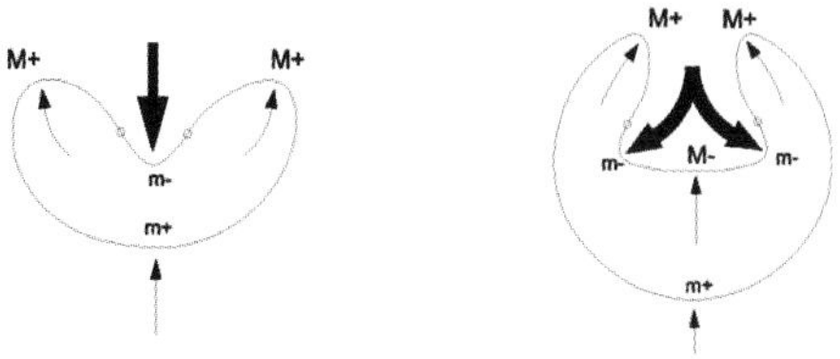

Figure 2.14: The downward arrow (left shape) branches to form a bay (right shape).

the center of the island. The mountain ridge acted as a resistance to the inflow of water, and thus the bay was formed. In the center of the bay, the point labelled M^- is a curvature extremum, because it is the point on the bay with the *least* amount of bend (i.e., extreme in the sense of "least").

Now, our concern here, with this resistance arrow, is the following: What happens when the process is continued along the direction of the arrow? This could happen, for example, if there is a volcano in the mountains that erupts, sending lava down into the sea. The result would therefore be the shape shown on the right of Fig. 2.12. In other words, a promontory would be formed into the sea.

3. SHIELD-FORMATION: This is illustrated in Fig. 2.13. Here the upward bold arrow, in the left shape, *branches*, to create a shield in the right shape, against the downward squashing process at the top of the right shape. Notice that the extremum M^+ at the top of the left shape has split into two copies of itself on either side of the right shape.

4. BAY-FORMATION: This is illustrated in Fig. 2.14. Here the downward bold arrow, in the left shape, *branches*, to create a bay in the right shape, against the upward resisting process in the center of the right shape. Notice that the extremum m^- at the center

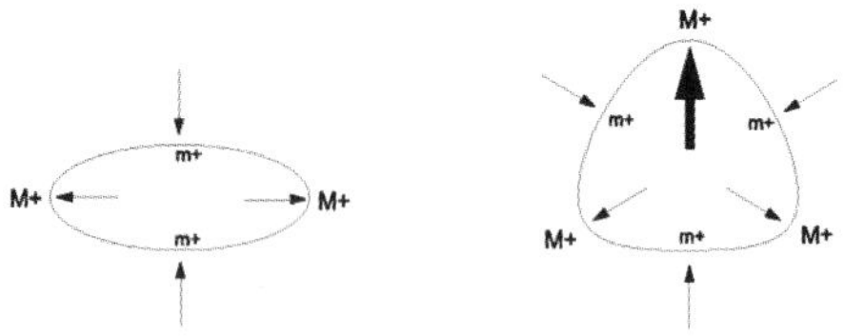

Figure 2.15: The main effect is the breaking-through of the upward bold arrow in the right shape. This has caused the downward squashing arrow in the left shape to split into two copies of itself, which move to the two sides of the right shape.

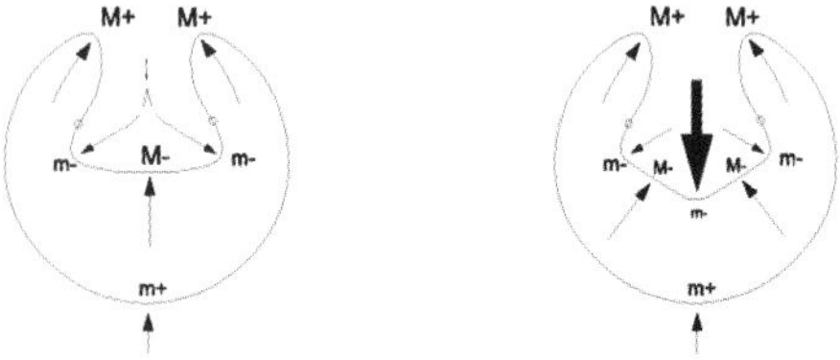

Figure 2.16: The main effect is the breaking-through of the downward bold arrow in the right shape. This has caused the upward resisting arrow in the center of the left shape to split into two copies of itself, which move to the two sides of the bay in the right shape.

of the left shape has split into two copies of itself on either side of the bay in the right shape.

5. Breaking-through of a protrusion: This is illustrated in Fig. 2.15. The situation starts with the left shape, where, at the top, there is the downward squashing arrow. This changes to the right shape where the upward bold protruding arrow has broken through. In breaking through, it has split the previous downward squashing arrow into two copies of itself, which have moved to either side of the shape; i.e. they are now seen as the two side arrows on the right shape.

6. Breaking-through of an indentation: This is illustrated in Fig. 2.16. The situation starts with the left shape, where, in the center of the bay, there is the upward resisting arrow. This changes to the right shape where the downward bold indenting arrow has broken through. In breaking through, it has split the previous upward resisting arrow into two copies of itself, which have moved to either side of the bay in the right shape.

Above, I have given the six types of events or operations, into which any deformation can be decomposed with respect to the effects at extrema. I call this the *Process-Grammar*. The six operations are listed in the table below. For each operation, the table first gives the intuitive description in English, and then the rigorous effect in terms of the curvature extrema involved. The rigorous definitions can be checked on the figures illustrating these operations.

PROCESS GRAMMAR

1. Squashing continues till it indents:	$m^+ \rightarrow 0m^-0$
2. Resistance continues till it protrudes:	$M^- \rightarrow 0M^+0$
3. Shield-formation:	$M^+ \rightarrow M^+m^+M^+$
4. Bay-formation:	$m^- \rightarrow m^-M^-m^-$
5. Breaking-through of a protrusion:	$m^+ \rightarrow m^+M^+m^+$
6. Breaking-through of an indentation:	$M^- \rightarrow M^-m^-M^-$

2.8 Process-Grammar and Asymmetry Principle

Now the following observation is fundamentally important: Each of the six rules of the Process Grammar represents an increase in asymmetry over time. This is because each increases the distinguishability in curvature – which is the asymmetry being studied here. To confirm this, observe that each of the right-hand shapes, in Figs. 2.11-2.16, fluctuates more than the corresponding left-hand shapes.

Mathematically, this is due to the fact that each of the operations in the Process-Grammar replaces one curvature symbol by a triple of curvature symbols – thus increasing the distinguishability. Therefore, we conclude: each of the six rules of the Process Grammar is an example of the Asymmetry Principle.

Now, recall my basic principle that memory is stored only in asymmetries. This leads to the following conclusion: *The six rules of the Process Grammar are the six possible ways in which memory storage can increase at curvature extrema.*

Finally, observe this: The purpose of this chapter has been to illustrate the fact that my new foundations for geometry give systematic rules for the extraction of memory from shape. In this chapter, the rules presented were those that extract memory from curvature extrema. However, my other books elaborate a system of several hundred rules that extract memory from other asymmetries in shape.

2.9 Scientific Applications of the Process-Grammar

A basic claim of my new foundations for geometry is that they give a unified basis for all the sciences and all the arts – i.e., the claim is that the sciences and the arts are all determined by the single goal of maximization of memory storage, and that this gives them an underlying mathematical equivalence.

Almost as soon as I published the Process-Grammar in the journal *Artificial Intelligence* (1988), scientists began to apply it in several disciplines; e.g., radiology, meteorology, computer vision, chemical engineering, geology, computer-aided design, anatomy, botany, forensic science, software engineering, urban planning, linguistics, mechanical engineering, computer graphics, art, semiotics, archaeology, anthropology, etc.

It is worth considering a number of applications here, to illustrate various concepts of the theory. In meteorology, Evangelos Milios used the Process-Grammar to analyze and monitor high-altitude satellite imagery in order to detect weather patterns. This allowed the identification of the forces involved; i.e., the forces go along the arrows. It then becomes possible to make substantial predictions concerning the future evolution of storms. This work was done in relation to the Canadian Weather Service.

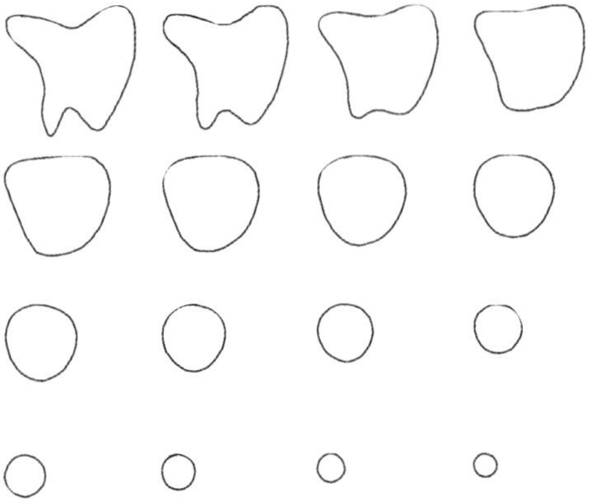

Figure 2.17: Continuous realization of the Process-Grammar for biological applications, by Steven Shemlon, using an elastic string equation.

It is also worth considering the applications by Steve Shemlon, in biology. Shemlon developed a continuous model of the grammar using an elastic string equation. For example, Fig. 2.17 shows the backward time-evolution, provided by the equation. It follows the laws of the Process-Grammar. Notice how the shape goes back to a circle, as predicted in section 2.5. Fig. 2.18 shows the corresponding tracks of the curvature extrema in that evolution. In this figure, one can see that the rules of the Process-Grammar mark the evolution stages. Shemlon applied this technique to analyze neuronal growth models, dental radiographs, electron micrographs and magnetic resonance imagery.
Let us now turn to an application by Jean-Philippe Pernot to the manipulation of free-form features in computer-aided design. Pernot's method begins by defining a limiting line for a feature as well as a target line. For example, the first surface in Fig. 2.19 has a feature, a bump, with a limiting line given by its oval boundary on the surface, and its target line given by the ridge line along the top of the bump. The Process-Grammar is then used to manipulate the limiting line of the feature. Thus, applying the first operation of the grammar to the left-hand squashing process m+ in the surface, this squashing continues till it indents

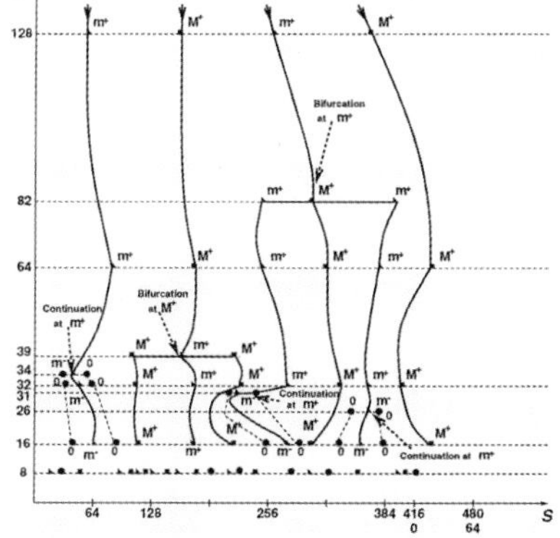

Figure 2.18: Shemlon's use of the Process-Grammar to label the transitions in the biological example in Fig. 2.17.

in the second surface shown in Fig. 2.19. With this method, the designer is given considerable control over the surface to produce a large variety of free-form features.

A profound point can be made by turning to the medical applications for illustration. Let us consider the nature of medicine. A basic goal of medicine is *diagnosis*. In this, the doctor is presented with the current state of, let's say, a tumor, and tries to *recover* the causal history which led to the current state. Using the terminology of this book, the doctor is trying to *convert* the tumor into a memory store. Generally, I argue: *Medicine is the conversion of biological objects into memory stores.*

Thus one can understand why the Process-Grammar has been used extensively in medical applications.

However, in section 4.2, I argue that all of science is the conversion of external physical objects into memory stores; in fact, that *science is the extension of the human computational system to encompass the environment as extra memory stores.*

With respect to this, it is particularly instructive to look at the application of the Process-Grammar to chemical engineering by John Peter Lee. Here the grammar was used to model molecular dynamics – in particular, the dynamical interactions within mixtures of solvent and solute particles. Fig. 2.20 represents the data shape, in *velocity space*, of a single solute molecule as it interacts with other molecules.

The initial data shape is given by a sphere (in velocity space). This is deformed by the successively incoming data in such a way that, at any time, one can use my curvature inference rules on the current shape, in order to infer the *history of the data*. In other words, one does not have to keep the preceding data – one can use the rules to *infer* it. Incidently, the lines in Fig. 2.20 correspond to the axes associated with curvature extrema as predicted by the rules.

Lee stated that the advantage of basing the system on my rules was that inference can be made as to how the shape-altering "data-forces" have acted upon the data shape over the time course, thus giving insight into the nature of the computational force itself. In this, Lee shows a particularly deep understanding of my work. As I say in section 4.4, because the inference rules give a method of converting objects into memory stores, they give a method of *extending the computational system to include those objects as memory stores.*

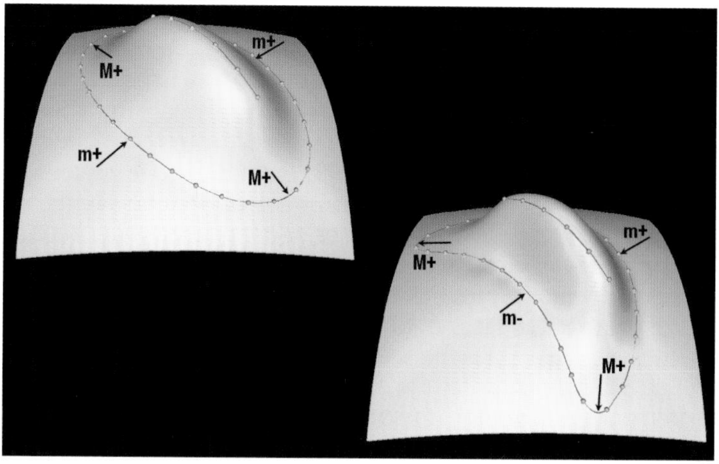

Figure 2.19: Application of the Process-Grammar to computer-aided design by Jean-Pilippe Pernot.

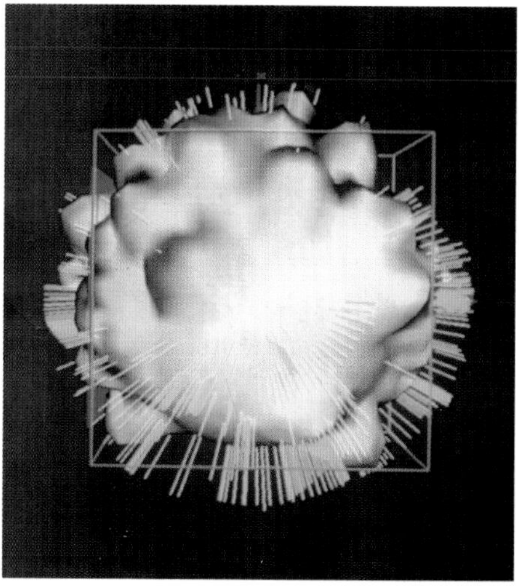

Figure 2.20: Application of the Process-Grammar to molecular dynamics by John Peter Lee.

2.10 Artistic Applications of the Process-Grammar

In section 2.9, we saw that the Process-Grammar has been applied in several scientific disciplines. In fact, Chapter 4 shows that the new foundations for geometry give a basis for the sciences *and the arts*. Thus, in my book the *Structure of Paintings*, I show the power of the grammar to reveal the compositions of paintings. In fact, the main argument of that book is this: *Paintings are structured by the rules of memory storage. That is, the rules of artistic composition are the rules of memory storage.* The book demonstrates this by giving detailed and lengthy analyses of paintings by Picasso, Modigliani, Gauguin, Holbein, Ingres, Balthus, Raphael, Cezanne, De Kooning, etc.

In Fig. 2.21, the rules for the extraction of history from curvature extrema are applied to Picasso's *Still Life*. The reader can see that this gives considerable insight into the composition of the painting.

Figure 2.21: Curvature extrema and their inferred processes in Picasso's Still Life.

2.11 Architectural Applications of the Process-Grammar

The Process-Grammar was a significant tool used in the creation of my Administration Buildings, some of which are shown in this book. To illustrate this in detail, we will look at the Fourth Administration Building, shown in Fig. 2.28.

Much of the generation of the building was based on two related sequences of operations which I call (1) the *Deepened-Bay Scenario*, and (2) the *Double-Bay Scenario*. Both sequences come from the Process-Grammar. We will examine them in turn:

(1) THE DEEPENED-BAY SCENARIO.

This scenario starts with a single extremum shown in Fig. 2.22a. In accord with my Symmetry-Curvature Duality Theorem, the extremum has a single process-arrow as shown. In the next stage, this arrow branches, forming a bay as shown in Fig. 2.22b. This is the use of operation 4, from the Process-Grammar, i.e., *bay-formation*. Notice that this involves not only the branching effect, but also the introduction of the upward process that creates the flattening in the center of the bay.

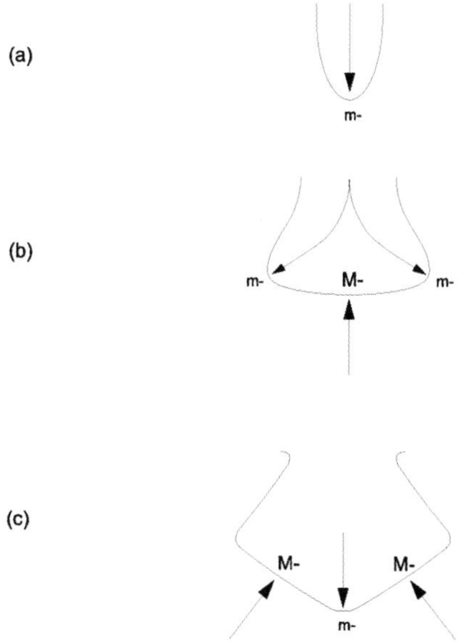

Figure 2.22: The Deepened-Bay Scenario.

Figure 2.23: The lower curve is an example of stage 1, a single extremum, in the Deepened Bay Scenario. The upper curve is an example of stage 2, the ordinary bay. (Fourth Administration Building.)

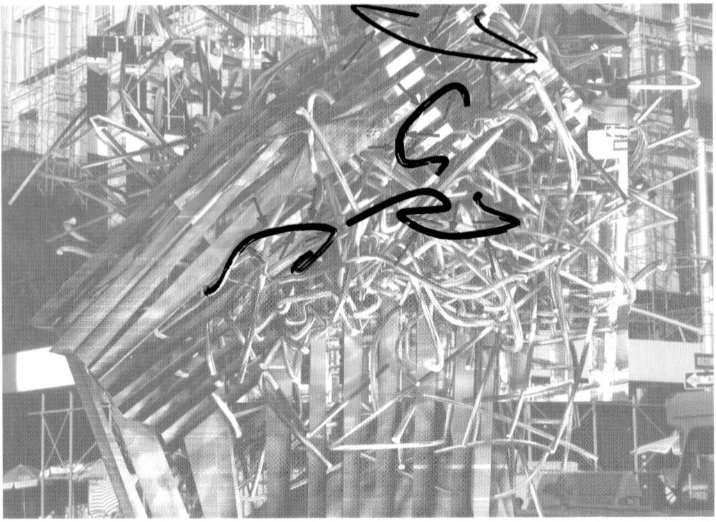

Figure 2.24: Four Deepened bays in the Fourth Administration Building.

Next, there is a breaking-through of the central downward plunging arrow, in Fig. 2.22c. This splits the previous upward arrow into two copies that go left and right. The event is the use of operation 6, from the Process-Grammar, i.e., breaking through of an indentation. The resulting shape shown in Fig. 2.22c is called the *deepened bay*.

The three-stage sequence in Fig. 2.22, which I call the Deepened-Bay Scenario, is used prolifically throughout my Fourth Administration Building. For instance, the lower curve in Fig. 2.23 shows an example of the first stage, the single extremum. Then, the upper curve in Fig. 2.23 shows the branching of the single extremum into the ordinary bay, i.e., the second stage of the scenario. Finally, Fig. 2.24 shows four examples of the deepened bay, i.e., the third stage. The reader will be able to identify over a hundred examples of this three-stage scenario in this administration building (Fig. 2.28).

(2) THE DOUBLE-BAY SCENARIO.

Here we start with *two* extrema, in opposite directions as shown in Fig. 2.25a. In the next stage, one of these two extrema is pre-

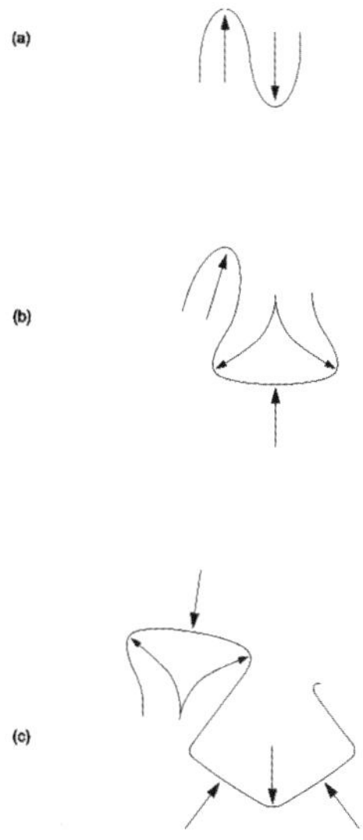

Figure 2.25: The Double-Bay Scenario.

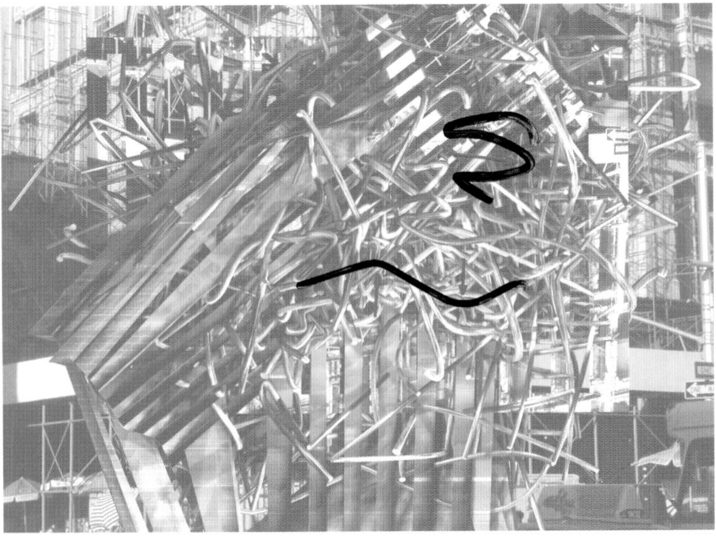

Figure 2.26: The lower curve has a double extremum. The upper curve takes this double extremum and preserves one extremum while branching the other to form a bay. (Fourth Administration Building.)

served – the left one in Fig. 2.25b – and the other branches to become a bay – the right part of Fig. 2.25c. Therefore, this stage is created by the application of the 4th Process-Grammar operation (bay-formation) to one of the two starting extrema. Notice that the other extremum might swing around to compensate, as seen on the left in Fig. 2.25b.

The third stage is shown in Fig. 2.25c. Here, two things have happened: (1) The previously preserved extremum – the left one in stage 2 – has now undergone branching, i.e., bay-formation, which is the 4th Process-Grammar operation. (2) The bay of stage 2 – on the right – has now undergone the transformation into a deepened bay; i.e., breaking-through of indentation, which is the 6th operation of the Process-Grammar.

The three-stage scenario in Fig. 2.25, which I call the Double-Bay Scenario, is used prolifically throughout my Fourth Administration Building. For example, the lower curve in Fig. 2.26 is an example of the first stage – a curve with the two extrema facing

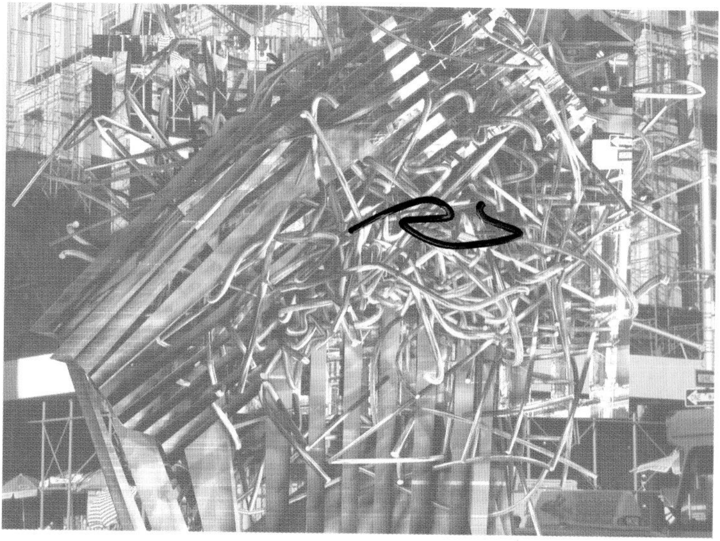

Figure 2.27: Then the preserved extremum in the previous curve is branched to form a bay, and the bay in the previous curve is branched to form a deepened bay. (Fourth Administration Building.)

in opposite directions. Then the upper curve in Fig. 2.26 preserves one of the extrema, while bifurcating the other into an ordinary bay, i.e., the second stage in the scenario. Finally, Fig. 2.27 shows the third stage. That is, the preserved extremum in the previous stage is branched into a bay, and the bay in the previous stage is branched into a deepened bay[1]. The reader will be able to identify many examples of this three-stage scenario in the Fourth Administration Building (Fig. 2.28).
In addition, Fig. 2.29 to Fig. 2.31 show three further versions of the Fourth Administration Building – all using multiple examples of the Deepened-Bay Scenario and Double-Bay Scenario.

1. Because the bays face in opposite directions, one of them is rigorously a shield, in the sense used in the Process-Grammar. This merely involves the figure-ground reversal of part of the above scenario.

Figure 2.28: The Fourth Administration Building, first version.

ONE

Figure 2.29: The Fourth Administration Building, second version.

Figure 2.30: The Fourth Administration Building, third version.

Figure 2.31: The Fourth Administration Building, fourth version.

Chapter 3
Architecture as Maximal Memory Storage

3.1 Introduction

My argument is that architecture up till now has been concerned with the minimization of memory storage, whereas the architecture I am proposing is concerned with the maximization of memory storage. This opposition exactly corresponds to the opposition between the conventional foundations for *geometry* (which concern the minimization of memory storage) and my new foundations for geometry (which concern the maximization of memory storage). As stated in section 1.1: *New foundations to geometry mean new foundations to architecture*.
The purpose of this chapter is to show more deeply how memory storage can be increased in architecture.

3.2 The Two Fundamental Principles

In my book *A Generative Theory of Shape*, I argue that maximization of memory storage requires the fulfillment of two fundamental principles: The first is this:

> MAXIMIZATION OF RECOVERABILITY. Maximize the retrievability of past states.

The means by which retrievability is made possible has been shown in Chapters 1 and 2. For example, we saw that past states are retrievable only from asymmetries.
However, I also argue that the maximization of memory storage is based on another principle, *maximization of transfer*, which means this: A situation is not seen as new, but as the transfer of a previous situation. Note that it is a basic cognitive fact about human beings that they see any situation they encounter in terms of previous situations. This is an essential way in which the cognitive system makes sense of the world. It allows previous solutions to be adapted to new situations.
To see a situation *B*, not as new, but as the transfer of a previous situation *A*, is to represent *B* as a memory store for *A*. In fact, as explained later, we will not describe transfer in terms of "situations" but in terms of actions – a set of actions is transferred

from one part of the history to another part of the history. However, observe that the process of transfer must itself be carried out by a set of actions. Therefore, in transfer, there are two levels of actions: the set of actions being transferred, and the set of actions doing the transfer. Now, since these two sets of actions constitute history that the object undergoes, we have this:

> Transfer is the history of history

The maximization of transfer is therefore expressed like this:

> MAXIMIZATION OF TRANSFER. Maximize the transfer of history by history.

The profound relationship between transfer and memory storage will be defined in this chapter.

3.3 Groups

The phenomenon of transfer will be analyzed using the mathematical concept of a *group*.

> A group is a complete system of transformations.

Examples of groups are:

> (1) ROTATIONS. The complete system of rotations around a circle.
> (2) TRANSLATIONS. The complete system of translations along a line.
> (3) DEFORMATIONS. The complete system of deformations of an object.

The word "complete" is defined as follows: Let us suppose we can list the collection of transformations T_i in a group G, thus:

$$G = \{T_0, T_1, T_2, \ldots\}.$$

For example, the transformations T_i might be rotations. The condition that this collection is *complete*, means satisfying the following three properties:

(1) Closure. For any two transformations in the group, their combination is also in the group. For example, if the transformation, *rotation by 30°*, is in the group, and the transformation, *rotation by 60°*, is in the group, then the combination, *rotation by 90°*, is also in the group.

(2) Identity Element. The collection of transformations must contain the "null" transformation, i.e., the transformation that has no effect. Thus, if the transformations are rotations, then the null transformation is *rotation by zero degrees*. Generally, one labels the null transformation e, and calls it the *identity element*. In the above list, we can consider T_0 to be the identity element.
(3) Inverses. For any transformation in the group, its inverse transformation is also in the group. Thus, if the transformation, *clockwise rotation by 30°*, is in the group, then its inverse, *anti-clockwise rotation by 30°*, is also in the group.
There is a fourth condition on groups, called associativity, which is so simple that it need not be considered here.

3.4 Generating a Shape by Transfer
As argued in section 3.2, the maximization of memory storage is dependent on satisfying two criteria: (1) maximization of recoverability, and (2) maximization of transfer. The previous chapters discussed recoverability. We now turn to transfer. The first thing we will do is illustrate the means of generating a shape by transfer. Fig. 3.1 shows a deformed cylinder. To generate it entirely by transfer, we proceed as follows:

STAGE 1. Create a single point in space.
STAGE 2. Transfer the point around space by rotating it, thus producing a circle. This is illustrated in Fig. 3.2.
STAGE 3. Transfer the circle through space by translating it, thus producing a straight cylinder. This is illustrated in Fig. 3.3.
STAGE 4. Transfer the straight cylinder onto the deformed cylinder by deforming it.

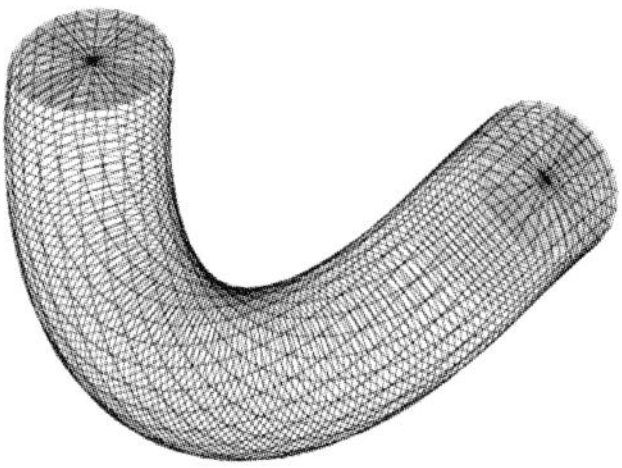

Figure 3.1: A deformed cylinder.

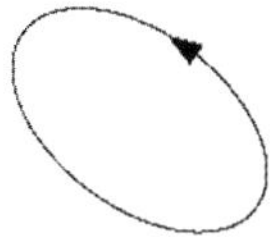

Figure 3.2: A point is transferred by rotations, producing a circle.

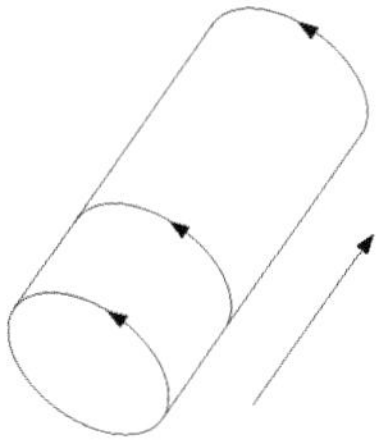

Figure 3.3: The circle is then transferred by translations, producing a straight cylinder.

Now observe that the four successive stages created a succession of four structures:

Point → Circle → Straight cylinder → Deformed cylinder.

Most importantly, observe that each of the successive stages created its structure by *transferring* the structure created at the previous stage; i.e., there is transfer of transfer of transfer. This means that the final object was created by a *hierarchy of transfer*. Furthermore, the transfer at each stage was carried out by applying a set of actions to the previous stage, thus:

Stage 2 applied the group ROTATIONS to Stage 1.
Stage 3 applied the group TRANSLATIONS to Stage 2.
Stage 4 applied the group DEFORMATIONS to Stage 3.

This hierarchy of transfer can be written as follows:

POINT Ⓣ ROTATION Ⓣ TRANSLATIONS Ⓣ DEFORMATIONS.

The symbol Ⓣ means "transfer." Each group, along this expression, transfers its left-subsequence, i.e., the entire sequence to its

left. That is, going successively, left-to-right along the sequence: (1) the group Rotations transfers its left-subsequence Point to create a circle; then (2) the group Translations transfers its left-subsequence Point Ⓣ Rotations (the circle) to create a straight cylinder, and finally, (3) Deformations transfers its left-subsequence Point Ⓣ Rotations Ⓣ Translations (the straight cylinder) to create the deformed cylinder.
It is important to notice that the hierarchical transfer structure means that there are no actual objects, only actions. For example, Fig. 3.3 shows that each cross-section is described as a circular action, and the relation between the cross-sections is described by a translational action. Thus, as stated earlier, transfer is a set of actions applied to a set of actions. That is:

> Transfer is the application of history to history; i.e., transfer is the history of history.

For example, the rotational history that produced the cross-section, itself undergoes a translational history.

3.5 Fiber and Control

Section 3.4 introduced the transfer operation Ⓣ. This operation always relates two groups, thus:

$$G_1 \text{ Ⓣ } G_2.$$

The lower group, that to the left of Ⓣ, is *transferred* by the upper group, that to the right of Ⓣ. The lower group will be called the fiber group; and the upper group will be called the control group. That is, we have:

Fiber Group Ⓣ Control Group.

The reason for this terminology can be illustrated with the straight cylinder. Here, the lower group was Rotations, which generated the cross-section, and the upper group was Translations, which transferred the cross-section along the cylinder, thus:

Rotations Ⓣ Translations.

The thing to observe is that this transfer structure causes the cylinder to decompose into *fibers*, the cross-sections, as shown in Fig. 3.4. Each fiber, a cross-section, is individually generated by the lower group ROTATIONS. It is for this reason that I call the lower group, the *fiber group*. Notice, also from Fig. 3.4, that the other group TRANSLATIONS, *controls* the position of the fiber along the cylinder. This is why I call the upper group, the *control group*.

Generally, a transfer structure causes a *fibering* of some space. As a further illustration, consider what happened when we created the deformed cylinder by adding DEFORMATIONS, above the straight cylinder thus:

ROTATIONS Ⓣ TRANSLATIONS Ⓣ DEFORMATIONS.

Here, DEFORMATIONS acts as a control group, and the group to its left, ROTATIONS Ⓣ TRANSLATIONS, acts as its fiber group. In this case, the fibers are now the various deformed versions of the cylinder. For example, the straight cylinder is the initial fiber, and any of its deformed versions (created by the control group), are also fibers.

In my mathematical work, I showed that the transfer operation Ⓣ can be powerfully modelled by the group-theoretic operation called a *wreath product*.

3.6 Projection as Memory

It is instructive now to consider the shape shown in Fig. 3.5. This is a square that has been projected onto a screen, i.e., it is *projectively distorted*. To generate it entirely by transfer, proceed as follows:

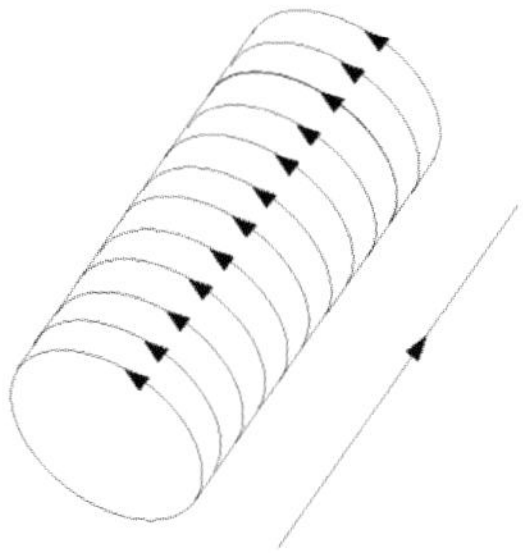

Figure 3.4: Under transfer, a cylinder decomposes into fibers.

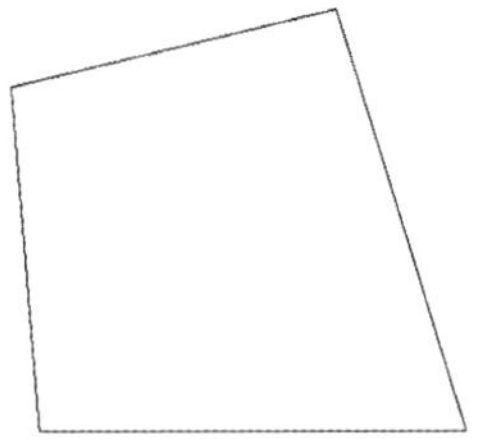

Figure 3.5: A square distorted by projection.

Figure 3.6: The generation of a side, using translations.

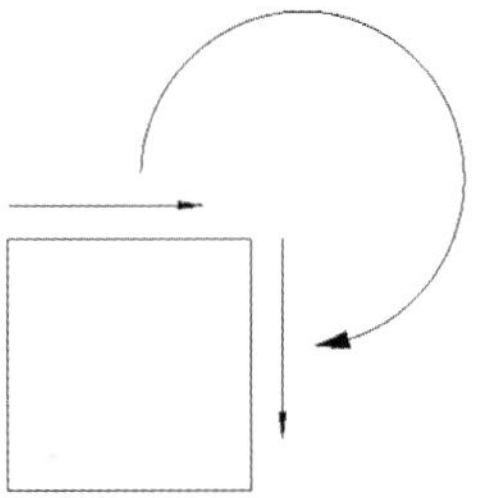

Figure 3.7: Transfer of translation by rotation.

STAGE 1. Create a single point in space.

STAGE 2. Transfer the point along a line by translating it, thus producing a straight line. This is shown in Fig. 3.6.

STAGE 3. Transfer the line by rotating it by 90° steps, thus producing a regular square. This is shown in Fig. 3.7.

STAGE 4. Transfer the regular square onto the distorted one, by projecting it. This produces the projectively distorted square in Fig. 3.5.

Observe that the four successive stages created a succession of four structures:

Point → Line → Regular Square → Distorted square.

Most importantly, each of the successive stages created its structure by *transferring* the structure created at the previous stage. This means that the final object was created, all the way up from a point, by transfer.
Let us introduce some terminology. The group used in Stage 3, rotating the side successively around the square, is the group of four successive 90° rotations. This group will be labelled 4-ROTATIONS. Then, the group used in Stage 4, creating the projectively distorted square from the regular square, is the group of projective transformations of an object. We will label this group, PROJECTIONS. It is called the *projective group*.
Now observe that the transfer, at each stage, was carried out by applying a set of actions to the previous stage, thus:

Stage 2 applied the group TRANSLATIONS to Stage 1.
Stage 3 applied the group 4-ROTATIONS to Stage 2.
Stage 4 applied the group PROJECTIONS to Stage 3.

This hierarchy of transfer can be written as follows:

POINT Ⓣ TRANSLATIONS Ⓣ 4-ROTATIONS Ⓣ PROJECTIONS.

Notice that the fiber, consisting of the first three levels:

POINT Ⓣ TRANSLATIONS Ⓣ 4-ROTATIONS

corresponds to the regular square.
The present section was given in order to show two things: (1) The projective process in perception can be described by transfer. For instance, in the above case, the regular square is transferred, as fiber, onto the projected square as fiber. Formulating projection as transfer gives a much more powerful mathematics than that encountered in current research in perceptual psychology and computer vision. (2) Because transfer is used to describe both the internal structure of objects, e.g., the internal structure of the regular square, and external actions applied to the object, such as projection, we have remarkable scientific unity across the two domains.

We should also note that projection acts to asymmetrize an object. Therefore, according to the Asymmetry Principle (section 1.5), a projected object stores the memory of the projective process; i.e., it is an increased memory store.

3.7 Regularity in Classical Architecture

Classical architecture is dominated by regular objects and regular arrangements. Examples include columns, lines of columns, reflectional sets of windows, etc. Using my new foundations for geometry, I will now give a theory of what regularity means, and then apply it to architecture:

> THEORY OF REGULARITY
>
> (1) The generative actions are structured as an *n*-fold hierarchy of transfer: $G_1 \textcircled{T} G_2 \textcircled{T} \ldots\ldots\ldots\ldots \textcircled{T} G_n$.
>
> (2) Each level can be specified by one parameter, e.g., angle around a circle, distance along a line. This parameter represents the parameter of time. Thus, the transfer hierarchy represents the *transfer of time by time*.
>
> (3) Each level consists of a group of actions that preserve shape and size. Mathematically, there are only three kinds of actions that preserve shape and size: translations, rotations, and reflections (together with their combinations). The mathematical term for such transformations is *isometries*.

It should be noted that, with respect to condition (2) above, a group given by one parameter can be specified by repeating a single generator. In the continuous case (e.g., continuous rotation around the circle), the generator is infinitesimal. In the discrete case (e.g., movement by regular steps along the ground), the generator is finite.

The class of groups satisfying the above three properties were invented by me in my mathematical research, and I call them ISO-REGULAR GROUPS. Let me give some illustrations:

Observe first that a straight cylinder is given by an iso-regular group:

$$\text{ROTATIONS} \quad \textcircled{T} \quad \text{TRANSLATIONS.}$$

That is, it satisfies the above three properties: (1) It is an *n*-fold hierarchy of transfer; (2) each level is specified by one parameter

(ROTATIONS specified by angle, and TRANSLATIONS by distance along a line); and (3) each level preserves shape and size.
In contrast, consider the deformed cylinder:

ROTATIONS Ⓣ TRANSLATIONS Ⓣ DEFORMATIONS.

This requires an extra level of transfer, the group DEFORMATIONS, which breaks conditions (2) and (3) of our theory of regularity: for example, DEFORMATIONS does not preserve shape and size. Therefore, whereas the transfer hierarchy for a straight cylinder is an iso-regular group (i.e., it satisfies all three conditions), the transfer hierarchy for a deformed cylinder is not an iso-regular group. I will say, in the latter case, that the added level (deformations) *breaks the iso-regularity*.
Now let us turn to the example of the square. Observe first that the regular square is given by an iso-regular group:

TRANSLATIONS Ⓣ 4-ROTATIONS.

That is, it satisfies the above three properties: (1) It is an *n*-fold hierarchy of transfer; (2) each level is specified by one parameter (TRANSLATIONS is specified by distance along a line, and 4-ROTATIONS by repeating the generator, 90°-rotation); and (3) each level preserves shape and size.
In contrast, consider the projectively distorted square:

TRANSLATIONS Ⓣ 4-ROTATIONS Ⓣ PROJECTIONS.

This requires an extra level of transfer, the group PROJECTIONS, which breaks conditions (2) and (3) of our theory of regularity: for example, PROJECTIONS does not preserve shape and size. Therefore, whereas the transfer hierarchy for a regular square is an iso-regular group (i.e., it satisfies all three conditions), the transfer hierarchy for a projectively distorted square is not an iso-regular group. I will say again that the added level (projections) *breaks the iso-regularity*.
The theory of regularity, given above, allows us to develop an understanding of regularity in classical architecture. I will argue:

REGULARITY IN CLASSICAL ARCHITECTURE
The regular surfaces and regular arrangements in classical architecture correspond to iso-regular groups.

Let us first consider regular surfaces in classical architecture. The claim that regular surfaces are given by iso-regular groups allows us to give a systematic classification of such surfaces. This classification is shown in Table 3.1, which we will now explain.
The term level-continuous means that all levels are continuous. Level-discrete means that at least one level is discrete. Consider first the level-continuous surfaces. Mathematically, it is known that there are only two continuous groups based on one parameter: (1) the group ROTATIONS around a point in a plane, and (2) the group TRANSLATIONS along a line. Since we want to maximize transfer, these primitives are generated simply by taking all possible 2-level transfer hierarchies using ROTATIONS and TRANSLATIONS.
Notice that the table gives the cylinder in two forms, which I call the *cross-section cylinder* and the *ruled cylinder*. These reverse the order of ROTATIONS and TRANSLATIONS.
The two versions are illustrated in Fig. 3.8. The cross-section cylinder is shown on the left, and is the transfer of the circular cross-section (fiber) along the axis (control). In contrast, the ruled cylinder is shown on the right, and is the transfer of a straight line (fiber), around the circular cross-section (control).
The lower half of the table gives what I call the level-discrete primitives. The cross-section block and ruled block correspond to the two cylinder cases just discussed, where the continuous rotation group ROTATIONS is replaced by the discrete group of *n* equal-

Level-Continuous	
Plane	TRANSLATIONS Ⓣ TRANSLATIONS
Sphere	ROTATIONS Ⓣ ROTATIONS
Cross-Section Cylinder	ROTATIONS Ⓣ TRANSLATIONS
Ruled Cylinder	TRANSLATIONS Ⓣ ROTATIONS
Level-Discrete	
Cross-Section Block	TRANSLATIONS Ⓣ *n*-ROTATIONS Ⓣ TRANSLATIONS
Ruled or Planar-Face Block	TRANSLATIONS Ⓣ TRANSLATIONS Ⓣ *n*-ROTATIONS
Cube	TRANSLATIONS Ⓣ TRANSLATIONS Ⓣ REFLECTION Ⓣ 3-ROTATIONS

Table 3.1: The regular surfaces of classical architecture are given by iso-regular groups.

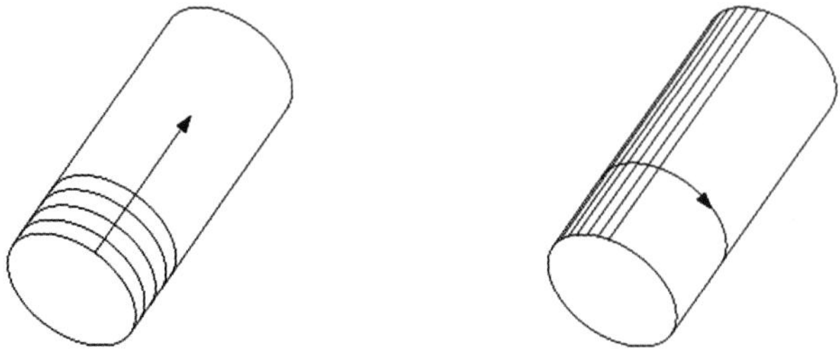

Figure 3.8: Two alternative ways of generating a cylinder

ly-spaced rotations around a center, called *n*-Rotations. The cross-section in the two types of block is an *n*-sided polygon, given by the component Translations Ⓣ *n*-Rotations in the entries shown for these two blocks in the table. Notice that Translations Ⓣ *n*-Rotations is the *n*-degree generalization of Translations Ⓣ 4-Rotations, given earlier for a square. The table shows that, in the cross-section block, the cross-section component Translations Ⓣ *n*-Rotations is the *fiber*, and Translations is the control that sweeps this through space. In the ruled block, these two components are reversed.

The final entry in the table is the cube. This is constructed as follows: The first two components, Translations Ⓣ Translations, define a plane, i.e., the face of a cube. The next component, Reflection, creates a pair of reflectionally opposite faces from this. The final component, 3-Rotations, generates all three pairs of opposite faces of the cube, by rotating them onto each other.

Now let us turn to regular *arrangements* in architecture. The rules are still the same: that is, I argue that regular arrangements are given by iso-regular groups. To illustrate, let us consider arrangements of columns. However the entire argument to be given applies to all the arrangements in classical architecture.

We have seen that a column is given by an iso-regular group, which we can assume is the ruled-cylinder Translations Ⓣ Rotations. A colonnade, shown in Fig. 3.9, is the *transfer* of a column by successive equal translations, i.e., by the group Equal-Translations. Therefore, the entire group of the colonnade is the following hierarchy of transfer:

Translations Ⓣ Rotations Ⓣ Equal-Translations

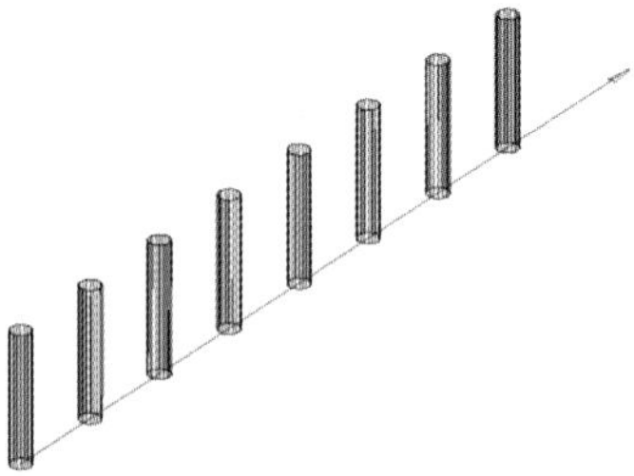

Figure 3.9: A colonnade as the transfer of a column by successive equal translations.

This is an iso-regular group. That is, (1) it is an *n*-fold hierarchy of transfer; (2) each level is specified by one parameter or generator; and (3) each level preserves shape and size.

Thus, we see that not only is a column given by an iso-regular group, but so is this standard *arrangement* of columns.

Now let us show that other arrangements of columns, in classical architecture, are given by iso-regular groups. Fig. 3.10 shows an arrangement of columns in Palladio's Villa Cornaro. Consider the arrangement of the six columns on the upper level. All columns are equally spaced from each other, except the middle two which are slightly further apart. In the figure, this can be seen clearly in the bottom set of columns, since this set does not have the additional guide-lines that have been placed on the top set.

The extra spacing between the two middle columns separates the left three columns from the right three columns as two visual groupings. Now consider the left three columns. It is reflectionally symmetric about the vertical line marked A. Similarly the right three columns are reflectionally symmetric about the line marked C. But observe that the central line marked B reflects the left three columns onto the right three columns. This means the reflection structure A, in the left grouping, is transferred onto the reflection structure C, in the right grouping, by the reflection structure B. In other words, the reflection structure A and the reflection structure C are two *fibers*, and the reflection structure B is the *control,* that sends the two fibers onto each other. That is, we get the transfer of reflection by reflection:

REFLECTION Ⓣ REFLECTION

Figure 3.10: The transfer of reflection by reflection, in Palladio's Villa Cornaro.

This, once again, is an iso-regular group. That is, (1) it is an *n*-fold hierarchy of transfer; (2) each level is specified by one parameter or generator; and (3) each level preserves shape and size. Therefore, again it illustrates my claim that the regularities of classical architecture are given by iso-regular groups.

The reader should note that Palladio uses this *reflection-transfers-reflection* structure not only for columns, but for other components such as windows. This can be seen, for example, by the arrangement of windows in the facade of this building, and in many of his other buildings. In fact, I have identified this as a frequent component of standard architecture. It is driven by having a centrally placed doorway, creating the control reflection group, and then organizing each individual half (to the left and right of the doorway) as a reflection structure in its own right, i.e., as a reflection fiber. Examples of this *reflection-transfers-reflection* structure range in diversity from St. Peter's in Rome to the Empire State Building in New York.

Let us return to Palladio's Villa Cornaro. The colonnade shown in Fig. 3.10 is at the *back* of the building, and this is itself reflected onto the colonnade at the *front* of the building. This means that there is a still higher level of transfer. That is, we add a further level of reflection onto the two-level reflection structure just given, thus obtaining a three-level transfer hierarchy of reflection:

REFLECTION Ⓣ REFLECTION Ⓣ REFLECTION

This, again, is an iso-regular group. In fact, let us now consider Palladio's Villa Rotunda. This building involves a major square

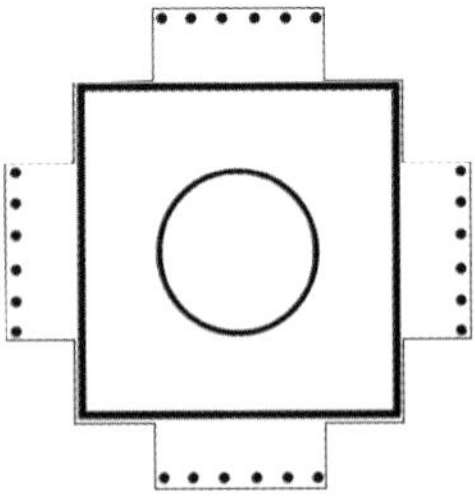

Figure 3.11: Plan of Palladio's Villa Rotunda.

floor-plan, as shown in Fig. 3.11. Furthermore, as seen in the figure, the six-column structure exists on each of the four sides. This can, of course, be modelled by adding the group of four rotations 4-ROTATIONS as the control group – transferring the six-column set successively around the four sides. Once again, this would be given by an iso-regular group. However, there is another iso-regular group that is equally relevant, and gives further insight into the situation, as follows: Fig. 3.12 shows three of the four reflection axes of a square. They are reflection m_V about the vertical axis, reflection m_H about the horizontal axis, and reflection m_D about one of the diagonal axes. The important thing to observe is this: The diagonal reflection *transfers* the vertical reflection onto the horizontal reflection. This transfer structure is critical. It allows us to regard the vertical reflection and the horizontal reflection as *fibers*, and the diagonal reflection as *control*, that sends the two fibers onto each other.

Now return to the Villa Rotunda. The six-column structure of the front, combined with the six-column structure of the back, is given by the same three-level hierarchy of reflections as in the Villa Cornaro, which has the same combination of front and back. However, in the Villa Rotunda this combination is itself transferred onto the combination of the left and right sides. This is done by the diagonal reflection axis – in the same way that m_D transfers m_H onto m_V in Fig. 3.12. The diagonal reflection is therefore a still higher level of reflection. The Villa Rotunda is thus given by a four-level hierarchy of reflection – each reflection layer transferring the previous layer, thus:

REFLECTION Ⓣ REFLECTION Ⓣ REFLECTION Ⓣ REFLECTION

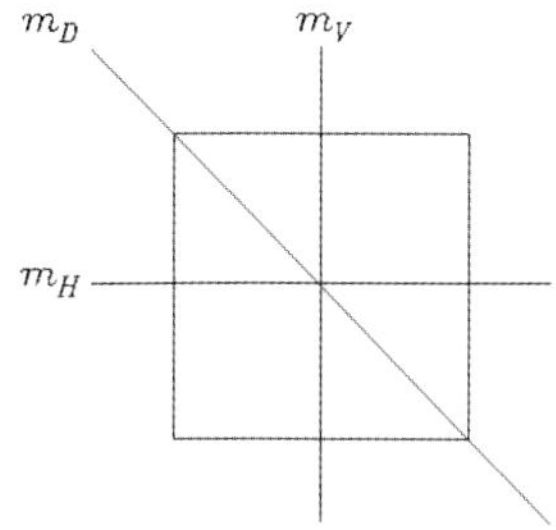

Figure 3.12: Transfer of reflection by reflection in a square.

Observe, once again, that this group is an iso-regular group, thus reinforcing my claim that regular structures in classical architecture are given by iso-regular groups.

3.8 Breaking the Iso-Regularity

We can now understand the enormous difference between the buildings discussed in the previous section, e.g., by Palladio, and my administration buildings shown in the plates of this book. Whereas the buildings of Palladio are structured by iso-regular groups, my adminstration buildings are not. Recall also that both the *components* (e.g., columns) and the *arrangements* of components (colonnades, etc.), in Palladio's buildings, are structured by iso-regular groups. In contrast, in my administration buildings, the components are highly deformed objects, and the arrangements are complex and highly irregular. In fact, since my buildings often involve extremely deformed cylinders, it is as if the colonnades of classical architecture have been mangled, broken, bludgeoned, twisted, and finally thrown into a pile as rejected garbage. Thank God, someone has taste! To the conventional aesthetic in architecture, my approach would be regarded very negatively. But, in the remainder of the book, we shall see its real value – first from a mathematical and computational point of view, and then from a psychological one.
At this stage, it is worth viewing the two approaches next to each other. For this, the reader should return to page 23, where Fig. 1.6 shows a colonnade of a classical administration building, and Fig. 1.7 shows what one can call a colonnade of one of my buildings. Architecture begins with the latter. Why?

The answer is that Palladio tries to minimize memory storage in a building, and I try to maximize it. Palladio is given the task of creating a set of rooms, and even though functional considerations might force the presence of some asymmetry, he will nevertheless try to minimize it, thus erasing memory as much as possible. In contrast, my purpose is to maximize the memory storage, and we have seen that this is done by breaking the iso-regular group, wherever possible.

It should be noted that, in my published mathematical work, I used this theory of iso-regular groups, and their breaking, to give a reformulation of the foundations of General Relativity and Quantum Mechanics. For example, the conservation laws of Special Relativity correspond to the iso-regular groups that are broken by General Relativity; and in Quantum Mechanics, the hierarchical description of an atom, through its fine and hyperfine splittings, correspond to the breaking of iso-regular groups.

3.9 Reference Frames

My published psychological work on perception has shown that the fundamental structure of the visual system is the Cartesian reference frame and that this is given by a *reflection* structure. For a 3D reference frame, the structure is as follows: Each of the three coordinate planes is visually understood as a reflection plane. These three reflection planes are three *fibers*, that are rotated onto each other by the order-3 rotation group, which acts as a *control* group. In fact, this transfer hierarchy is the same one as that given for the cube in Table 3.1. That is:

> The 3D Cartesian frame is given by an iso-regular group.
> This is the same iso-regular group as that of a cube.

We shall see that this is fundamental to the generation of buildings as maximal memory stores. My mathematical work has shown that most memory stores begin with the breaking of this iso-regular group.

3.10 New Theory of Symmetry-Breaking

The Asymmetry Principle states that recoverability of history is possible only if each asymmetry in the present goes back to a past symmetry. This means that, forward in time, the history must have been symmetry-breaking. That is, according to my

new foundations for geometry, *memory-stores are created only by symmetry-breaking*.
The new foundations present a new theory of symmetry-breaking, which will now be explained in order to understand how memory storage can be maximized in a building.
First, my new theory of symmetry-breaking opposes the theory that has dominated mathematics and physics for over a century. According to the standard theory, symmetry-breaking is described by reduction of a group, for the following reason: A symmetrical object is described by a group of transformations that send the figure to itself (e.g., reflections). In fact, the symmetries of the object are given by these transformations. When some of the symmetries are destroyed, then correspondingly some of those transformations are lost and, therefore, the group is reduced. This means a loss of information.
However, in our system, symmetry-breaking is associated with the expansion of the group. For instance, recall from section 3.4 the case of the cylinder. The straight cylinder was given by the group:

POINT Ⓣ ROTATIONS Ⓣ TRANSLATIONS

Then the deformed cylinder was given by taking this group as fiber, and extending it by the group DEFORMATIONS, via the transfer operation Ⓣ, thus:

POINT Ⓣ ROTATIONS Ⓣ TRANSLATIONS Ⓣ DEFORMATIONS

The added group, DEFORMATIONS, breaks the symmetry of the straight cylinder. However, the group of the straight cylinder is not lost in the above expression. It is retained as fiber. In fact, it is *transferred* onto the deformed cylinder, and it is this that allows us to see the latter cylinder as a *deformed version* of the straight cylinder. That is, the deformed cylinder *stores the memory* of the straight one.
Thus, we have a new view of symmetry-breaking:

NEW VIEW OF SYMMETRY-BREAKING. *When breaking the symmetry of an object which has symmetry group* G_1*, take this group as fiber, and extend it by the group* G_2*, via the transfer operation* Ⓣ*, thus:*

$$G_1 \; Ⓣ \; G_2$$

where G_2 is the group of the asymmetrizing action. As a result, we have this: The present is seen as a transferred version of the past.

3.11 Maximizing Memory Storage

In section 3.2, I argued that the maximization of memory storage requires two principles: (1) maximizing the recoverability of the past, and (2) maximizing the transfer of history by history. I will now show that there is a deep connection between these two principles.

Let us go back to the example of the deformed cylinder. Section 3.4 showed how this cylinder can be generated, all the way up from a point, by layers of transfer: One starts with a point, then one transfers the point by rotations to create a circle, then one transfers the circle by translations to create a straight cylinder, and finally one transfers the straight cylinder by deformations to produce the deformed cylinder. This means that, forward in time, one goes through a sequence of four stages that create a succession of four structures:

FORWARD TIME

Point → Circle → Straight cylinder → Deformed cylinder

Each stage creates its structure by transferring the structure created in the previous stage.

Now let us consider how one *recovers* that history. This means that one must reverse the arrows; i.e., go backward in time.

BACKWARD TIME

Deformed cylinder → Straight cylinder → Circle → Point

Thus, starting with the deformed cylinder *in the present*, one must *recover* the backward history through these stages. We now ask how this recovery of the past is possible. The answer comes from our Asymmetry Principle (section 1.5), which says that, to ensure recoverability of the past, any asymmetry in the present must go back to a symmetry in the past.

Now the word asymmetry, in mathematics and physics, really means *distinguishability*, and the word symmetry really means *indistinguishability*. Thus the Asymmetry Principle really says that, to ensure recoverability, any distinguishability in the present must go back to an indistinguishability in the past. In fact, the backward-time sequence, given above, is recovered exactly in this way, as follows:

(1) DEFORMED CYLINDER → STRAIGHT CYLINDER: The deformed cylinder has distinguishable (different) curvatures at different points on its surface. By removing these distinguishabilities (differences) in curvature, one obtains the straight cylinder, which has the same curvature at each point on its surface, i.e., indistinguishable curvature across its surface.

(2) STRAIGHT CYLINDER → CIRCLE: The straight cylinder has a set of cross-sections that are distinguishable by position along the cylinder. By removing this distinguishability in position for the cross-sections, one obtains only one position for a cross-section, the starting position. That is, one obtains the first circle on the cylinder.

(3) CIRCLE → POINT: The first circle consists of a set of points that are distinguishable by position around the circle. By removing this distinguishability in position for the points, one obtains only one position for a point, the starting position. That is, one obtains the first point on the circle.

We see, therefore, that each stage, in the backward-time direction, is recovered by converting a distinguishability into an indistinguishability. This means that each stage, in the forward-time direction, creates a distinguishability from an indistinguishability in the previous stage. Let us check this with the example of the deformed cylinder. The sequence of actions used to generate the deformed cylinder from a point are:

POINT Ⓣ ROTATIONS Ⓣ TRANSLATIONS Ⓣ DEFORMATIONS

Observe that each level creates a distinguishability from an indistinguishability in the previous level. That is, ROTATIONS produces a cross-section by creating distinguishability in position for the single point on the previous level. Then TRANSLATIONS produces a straight cylinder by creating distinguishability in position for the single cross-section on the previous level. And finally, DEFORMATIONS produces a deformed cylinder by creating distinguishability in curvature on the surface of the straight cylinder of the previous level.

The fact that each level creates a distinguishability (asymmetry) from an indistinguishability (symmetry) in the previous level, means that each level is *symmetry-breaking* on the previous level. However, we have also seen that each level *transfers* the previous level. This is a fundamental point: *Each level must act by both symmetry-breaking and transferring its previous level.* To fully understand the importance of this point, let us state it within the main argument of this section:

> MAXIMIZATION OF MEMORY STORAGE
> Maximization of memory storage requires (1) maximizing the recoverability of the past, and (2) maximizing the transfer of history by history. This means that each stage of the history must fulfill two conditions: (1) It must be symmetry-breaking on the previous stage. (2) It must act by transferring the previous stage.
> That is, each stage must be a *symmetry-breaking transfer* of the previous stage.

The concept of symmetry-breaking transfer is fundamental to my new foundations for geometry. It accords with the statement made at the end of section 3.10. Also it implies that, when one breaks a regularity, one does not lose the internal memory that was stored in it. That is, the actions generating the irregularity do not erase the previous regular actions in the memory store, but are actually *added* to the memory store. Therefore, the memory store increases.

The concept of symmetry-breaking transfer explains this phenomenon as follows: The actions creating the irregularity *transfer* the actions creating the regularity onto the irregularity. As an example, the actions that deform a regular cylinder transfer the regular cylinder onto the deformed cylinder. In other words, there is an "imprint" of the regular cylinder on the deformed cylinder. This means that the deformation was a *symmetry-breaking transfer* – i.e., it broke the symmetry of the past regularity, but transferred it onto the current irregularity. This allows the recoverability of the entire history; i.e., we can recover both the actions that generated the past regularity and the actions that generated the current irregularity. Therefore, memory storage has been maximized.

Thus, one can see that the concept of symmetry-breaking transfer is fundamental to any architecture that tries to maximize memory storage in a building. This concept is basic to that given in the next section, which is the culminating concept in our theory of how to maximize memory storage in a building – the concept of *unfolding*.

3.12 Theory of Unfolding

We will now use the principles developed in the previous sections to develop a generative theory of *complex* shape, such that it becomes possible to create buildings of arbitrarily large memory storage.

It is first necessary to solve the fundamental problem of *combining* objects. Consider Fig. 3.13. Each of the two objects *individually* has a high degree of symmetry. However, the *combined* structure shown loses much of this symmetry; i.e., causes a severe reduction in symmetry group. For example, the continuous rotational symmetry of the cylinder is not retained in the *combined* structure of the cylinder and cube. We want to develop a group that encodes exactly what the eye can see. In particular, in the combined situation, one can *still* see the individual objects. Therefore, we want to develop a group of the concatenated structure in which the groups of the individual objects are preserved, and yet there is the extra information of concatenation.

The new foundations solve this problem in the following way: the generative history of the configuration starts out with the two independent objects, and therefore the group of this starting situation is given by the group

$$G_{cylinder} \ X \ G_{cube}$$

where the groups $G_{cylinder}$ and G_{cube} are the iso-regular groups of the two objects, and the symbol X means direct product, which, in group theory, always encodes the *independence* of the two groups on either side of the product symbol.

Now, by the maximization of transfer, this starting group, i.e., the direct product group shown above, must be transferred onto subsequent states in the generative history, and therefore it must be the *fiber* of a transfer hierarchy in which the control group creates the subsequent generative process. Let us denote the control group by CONTROL which we will take to be the group of translations and deformations of three-dimensional space. The full structure, fiber plus control, is therefore the following transfer hierarchy:

$$[G_{cylinder} \times G_{cube}] \quad Ⓣ \quad \text{CONTROL}$$

The way this group will act will be as follows: First, by our theory of recoverability, the control group must have an asymmetrizing effect. Thus, the initial copy of the fiber $G_{cylinder} \times G_{cube}$ must be the most symmetrical configuration possible. This exists only when the cube and the cylinder are coincident with their symmetry structures *maximally aligned*. This will be called the ALIGNMENT KERNEL. For example, their centers, reflection planes, rotation axes, must be maximally coincident.

Next, choose one of the two objects to be a reference object. This will remain fixed at the origin of the coordinate system. Let us choose the cube as the referent.

Given this, now describe the action of the control group CONTROL translating and deforming the cylinder relative to the cube. Each subsequent copy of the fiber will therefore be some configuration of this system. The crucial concept is that the control group *transfers configurations onto configurations*.

Let us now understand how to add a further object, for example a sphere. First of all, the fiber becomes:

$$G_{sphere} \times G_{cylinder} \times G_{cube}$$

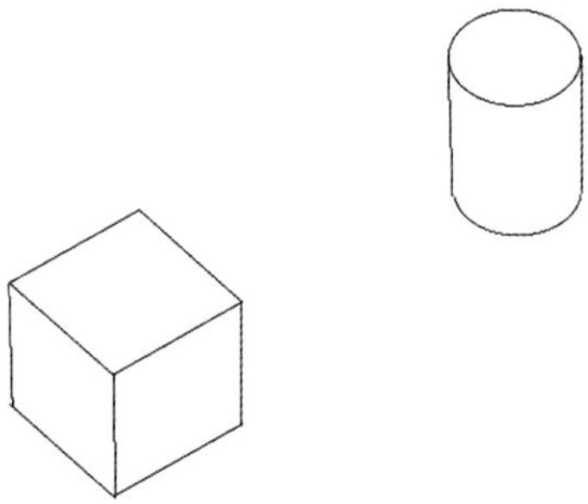

Figure 3.13: Combination breaks symmetry.

where we have added the iso-regular group of the sphere. In such expressions, our rule will be that each object encoded along this sequence provides the reference for its left-subsequence of objects. Thus the cube is the referent for the cylinder-and-sphere, and the cylinder is the referent for the sphere. Accordingly, there are now two levels of control, each of which is CONTROL, and each of which is added via the transfer product Ⓣ. Thus we obtain the 3-level transfer hierarchy:

$$[G_{sphere} \times G_{cylinder} \times G_{cube}] \circledT \ \mathrm{CONTROL}_1 \ \circledT \ \mathrm{CONTROL}_2$$

This is interpreted in the following way: Initially, the three objects (cube, cylinder, sphere) are coincident with their symmetry structures maximally aligned. This is the fiber copy I have called *the alignment kernel*. The higher control group $\mathrm{CONTROL}_2$ moves the cylinder-sphere pair in relation to the cube. The lower control group $\mathrm{CONTROL}_1$ moves the sphere in relation to the cylinder.
The above discussion has been illustrating a class of groups I invented, called TELESCOPE GROUPS. To get an intuitive sense of a telescope group, think of an ordinary telescope. In an ordinary telescope, you have a set of rings that are initially maximally coincident. Then you pull them successively out of alignment with each other. A telescope group is a group structured like this. In fact, it is part of a still larger class of groups which I invented, called UNFOLDING GROUPS. Unfolding groups are the most important class of generative structures in my new foundations for geometry. The basic idea is that any complex structure can be *unfolded* from a maximally collapsed version of itself which I call the alignment kernel.
Unfolding groups are characterized by the following two properties:

SELECTION: The control group acts *selectively* on only part of its fiber.
MISALIGNMENT: The control group acts by *misalignment*.

My published mathematical work has invented three kinds of unfolding groups that are particularly valuable in the creation of memory stores:

(1) Telescope groups.
(2) Super-local unfoldings.
(3) Sub-local unfoldings.

We have so far described the first type, telescope groups. Now let us move on to the second type, super-local unfoldings. These add an extra control level *above* the existing hierarchy such that it affects only some part of that hierarchy. These groups are useful because they can model cross-hierarchy selection and modification; i.e., they can cut across the existing hierarchy without respecting its boundaries, e.g., they can fracture the entire design. The third type, sub-local unfoldings, add an extra fiber level *below* only some part of the existing hierarchy. They can be regarded as generalizations of telescope groups. Intuitively, if a telescope group is regarded as an octopus with one arm, then a sub-local unfolding group can be regarded as an octopus with several arms; indeed the arms can themselves have arms, and so on.

An important result of defining sub-local unfoldings was that it allowed me to give an extensive algebraic theory of software. For example, I showed that such unfoldings provide a deep understanding of designer-created *inheritance*, which is a basic part of CAD, robotics, and animation. For instance, in designing a serial-link manipulator (like an arm), one specifies an inheritance hierarchy in which each link is the parent of the link below, which becomes its child. This means that the child link inherits the transform applied to its parent, but then adds its own. I gave the first algebraic theory of inheritance, showing that it is best formulated as a transfer (i.e., wreath) product of groups in which the child corresponds to the fiber and the parent corresponds to the control. This has a crucial relation to my theory of memory storage, as follows: Recall from section 3.9 that I proposed that a frame is actually a symmetry structure. Initially, in the design process, all object-frames are coincident (i.e., in their default values), and the successive design actions move the frames out of alignment. Thus, by my geometric theory, the design process breaks the symmetries of a frame. In this way, I showed that inheritance is given by *symmetry-breaking transfer*, which is the fundamental requirement given in section 3.11 for maximizing memory storage.

Also, I showed that sub-local unfoldings give a new formulation of the Boolean operations: All three Boolean operations are generated by an unfolding group.

A further powerful property of unfoldings is that they handle anomalies. This leads to the following understanding of complex shape: *Complex-shape generation is the generation of anomalies.*

Figs. 3.16-3.20 illustrate the mathematical principles of this section with some of my Administration Buildings, as follows:

FIRST ADMINISTRATION BUILDING.

The First Administration Building, shown in Fig. 3.16, was created by unfolding groups based on an alignment kernel containing two iso-regular groups: the world frame (as triple-reflection structure) and the cylinder. This means that, initially, the symmetries were maximally aligned, and unfolding successively misaligned the symmetries, thus creating the building as a memory store. For example, sub-local unfolding selected the horizontal reflection plane from the world-frame triple and rotated it, creating the fan of large planes shown in the center of the building – thus breaking the symmetry of the world frame. Furthermore, above this sub-local unfolding, a telescope unfolding group was then added, successively moving the rotation axis of the fan in the same way that the rotation axis of a joint undergoes successive Euclidean motions down the successive joints of a serial-link manipulator. This successive movement of rotation joints is shown along the bottom of Fig. 3.14.

SECOND ADMINISTRATION BUILDING.

The Second Administration Building, shown in Fig. 3.17, was created by unfolding groups based on an alignment kernel of three iso-regular groups – the cube, cylinder, and sphere – all aligned with the worldframe (which is an example of the cube as triple-reflection structure). This means that, initially, their symmetries were all maximally aligned, and unfolding successively misaligned these symmetries, thus creating the building as a memory store.

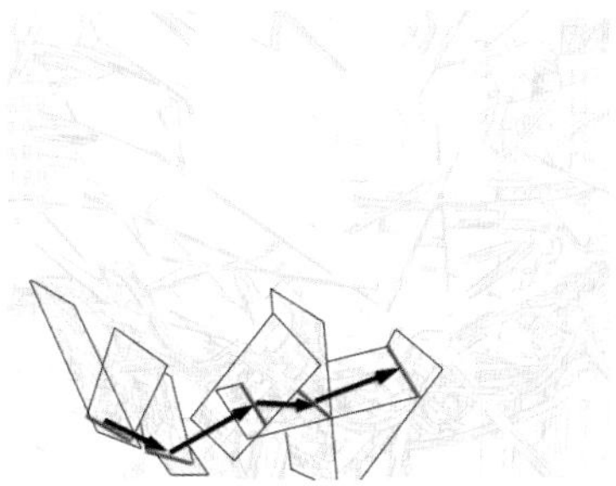

Figure 3.14: Succession of moved rotation axes in the First Administration Building.

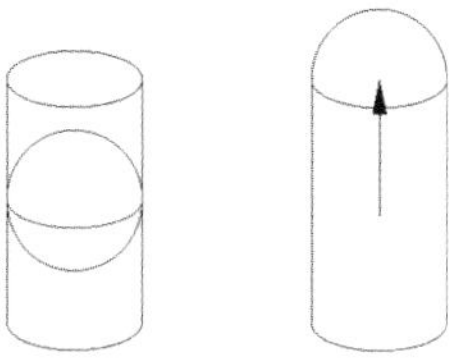

Figure 3.15: (a) Initially, the cylinder-sphere pair share the same horizontal reflection plane. (b) Unfolding has the effect of misaligning those reflection planes.

For example, the cube was unfolded out of alignment to become the set of four adjacent boxes shown in the middle (Fig. 3.17), which correspond roughly to four quadrants of the world frame. Then, they were successively misaligned further outwards from these four positions, to create successively increasing anomalies (broken cubes, dislodged planes, etc.). This is an example of sub-local unfolding. Also, within each unfolded box, there is a set of tubes which inherit (as parent to child) the position of the box but then undergo their own personal process of anomalization as inheritance children.

In addition, along the bottom, there are streams of cylinders that were unfolded as inheritance chains, independently from those tubes created within the boxes. The level of detail with which the theory works is considerable. For example, each tube along the bottom is an example of a *telescope group*, as follows: Each is a parent-child pair consisting of a cylinder (parent) and a sphere (child). Initially, the cylinder and sphere have their symmetries maximally aligned, as shown in Fig. 3.15a, where they share the same horizontal reflection plane through the center of the cylinder and the equator of the sphere. Fig. 3.15a, therefore, shows the *alignment kernel*. Then, the sphere is unfolded out to one end of the cylinder, as shown in Fig. 3.15b, thus misaligning their horizontal reflection planes. Notice that the transition from Fig. 3.15a to 3.15b has the *telescope-opening* effect that is basic to a telescope group.

THIRD ADMINISTRATION BUILDING.

Like the First Administration Building, the Third Administration Building, shown in Fig. 3.18, was created by unfolding groups based on an alignment kernel containing two iso-regular groups: the world frame and cylinder. However, whereas in the first building, sub-local unfolding was applied to the *horizontal* reflection plane from the triple reflection structure of the world frame, here, in contrast, unfolding was applied to all three planes. The planes shown in Fig. 3.18, therefore, represent a dislodged version of the original Cartesian frame; i.e., *the building is actually a comment on the world frame*, and it is so by having injected memory storage into that frame.

Fig. 3.19 illustrates some additional concepts using the Third Administration Building. First, a typical part of New York City was developed further using sub-local unfoldings, as follows: It should be noted that an ordinary apartment building has highly regular sub-structures (e.g., repeating windows) corresponding to iso-regular groups. In Fig. 3.19, perspective transformations were applied to such buildings. These transformations increase the memory storage because, as was shown in section 3.6, projection causes asymmetrization of iso-regular groups, thus ensuring the recoverability of the projective action. Notice that these projections were applied *sub-locally*, i.e., to the individual apartment buildings, not to the global city-scape.

A final crucial stage was added to this unfolded structure: The Third Administration Building was Boolean-subtracted from it. In other words, the administration building was *carved out* of the city-scape. This building is, therefore, not present in any way as positive space. It is present only as memory, its imprint left on the world, as a virulent ghost, holding together the projectively polluted landscape with its dislocated grasp.

FOURTH ADMINISTRATION BUILDING.

The Fourth Administration Building was discussed in section 2.11, where it was shown as Fig. 2.28. With the ideas of the present chapter, we can discuss it further. This building was created by unfolding groups based on an alignment kernel containing two iso-regular groups: the world frame and cylinder. The actions applied to the cylinder were discussed in detail in section 2.11, where it was shown that they follow the Deepened-Bay and Double-Bay Scenarios, compiled from the Process-Grammar. In the present section, we will therefore discuss the actions on the other iso-regular group, the world frame. Whereas the First Administration Building applied sub-local unfolding to the *hori-*

zontal reflection plane from the triple-reflection structure of the world frame, the Fourth Administration Building applied sub-local unfolding to the *vertical* plane in that triple-reflection structure. This is a crucial psychological difference, because the horizontal and vertical planes have different relationships to the gravitational field – the horizontal plane is in stable equilibrium and the vertical plane is in unstable equilibrium. Now, the particular vertical plane, selected by sub-local unfolding, is shown as the flat back plane that directly faces the viewer in Fig. 2.28. As can be seen, it has undergone stretching to a rectangle, which, being an asymmetrization, has increased its memory storage. The sub-local unfolding is continued further, as follows: The plane is then contracted to a narrow long vertical rectangle which is repeated by the iso-regular group of equal translations and Boolean subtracted from the back plane to produce the sequence of repeated rectangular holes along that plane. The rectangular holes destroy the continuous translational symmetry across the plane, thus increasing the memory storage further. Next, this structure – the back plane together with its sequence of rectangular holes – undergoes unfolding through various types of misalignments involving shearing, rotation and bending – which produce the large structures in front of the plane. This substantially increases the memory storage. The reader should note that the particular storage involved is related to the history inferred from a rotated parallelogram, in Fig. 1.5.

At this stage, it is worth illustrating the use of *super*-local unfolding. Fig. 3.20 shows the same building at a further stage of development. The added stage is a super-local unfolding. The reader will recall that, in such an unfolding, an extra control group is placed above the existing transfer hierarchy, and, therefore, in its selective action, it can *cut across* the inheritance hierarchy, ignoring the borders within that hierarchy. This is exactly what has happened here. The version of the Fourth Administration Building discussed in the previous paragraph now undergoes various cross-hierarchy selections plus misalignments that completely violate the hierarchy. As the reader can see, this results in a strong sense of fracturing. This asymmetrization has further increased the memory storage.

Figure 3.16: The First Administration Building.

Figure 3.17: The Second Administration Building.

Figure 3.18: The Third Administration Building.

Figure 3.19: A further development of the Third Administration Building.

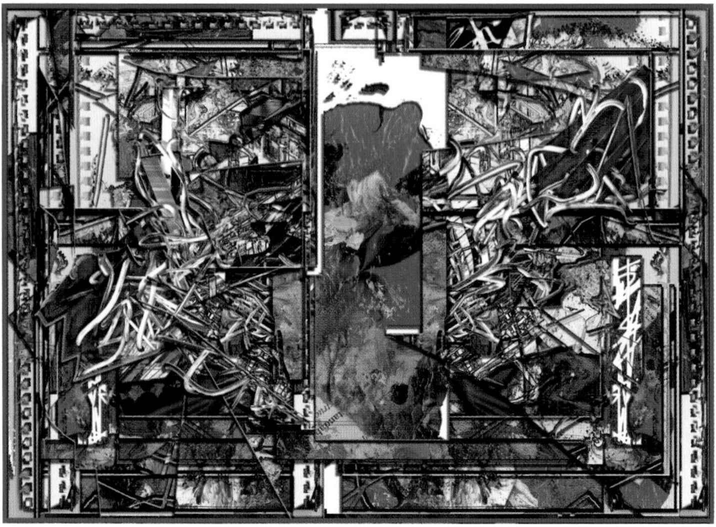

Figure 3.20: A further development of the Fourth Administration Building.

Chapter 4
Architecture and Computation

4.1 Introduction

My new foundations for geometry give a relationship between architecture and computation that is entirely different from the relationship that is standardly discussed. The standard relationship concerns the use of computers in architecture – both as tools for imaginative design, and also enabling manufacturing and construction. In this, the computer's role is one of facilitation. However, it is actually dispensable. Theoretically, it is possible to construct the buildings without the use of computers – except that this would take considerably longer. Therefore, what is used here is the standard property of a computer: speed based on miniaturization of a symbolic process – a process which could be carried out with a pencil and paper, and indeed was carried out with a pencil and paper in Turing's original formulation of a computer.

However, in contrast to this, my foundations of geometry define an entirely new relationship between architecture and computation. This relationship is not dispensable. In order to understand the new relationship, it is necessary to understand that the new theory of geometry gives new foundations for each of the following three areas: science, art, and computation. These will be described, successively, in the following sections.

4.2 New Foundations for Science

As a result of the new foundations for geometry, I have, in my mathematical research, been able to give new foundations for science. According to these foundations, *science is the conversion of objects into memory stores*. Let us illustrate this with general relativity and quantum mechanics.

In general relativity, empty space-time is flat. However, when one introduces mass, e.g., a planet, the resulting gravitational force causes space-time to become curved. We shall now see that this conforms with our Asymmetry Principle (section 1.5), which says that memory is stored only in asymmetries: The flatness of empty space-time is the most *symmetrical* condition possible. Then, the introduction of the gravitational force causes space-time to lose this symmetry, i.e., it becomes curved. Therefore, the asymmetry in curved space-time acts as a *memory store* for the action of the gravitational force.

Now let us turn to quantum mechanics. Consider, for example, the modelling of the hydrogen atom. The atom involves a number of forces between components of the electron and proton. The way this is modelled is as follows. One starts with the free-particle situation – that in which there is no force. Here, the potential energy is zero throughout space. This is the most symmetrical situation possible. That is, the potential energy is symmetric (indistinguishable) under translations across space and rotations around any point in space. Then one adds the most important force of the hydrogen atom – the electrostatic interaction between the electron and proton. This makes the situation *asymmetrical*. The reason is that the electrostatic force destroys the translational symmetry of the energy across space, as well as the rotational symmetry around any point, except the center of the atom. Then, in the next stage, one adds the force between the electron's spin and orbital angular momentum. This makes the energy still more asymmetrical. Then, in the next stage, one adds the force between the spins of the proton and electron. This makes the energy still more asymmetrical.

Thus, the successively added forces have the effect of successively adding asymmetries. Therefore, the successive asymmetries act as *memory stores* for the successive forces.

The above discussion has illustrated one of the basic principles of my new foundations for science: The purpose of science is to convert environmental objects into memory stores. This gives a deep analysis of scientific activity, as follows: Conventionally, one says that the main concern of science is explaining how things are caused. However, my book *Symmetry, Causality, Mind* (MIT Press, 630 pages) shows that "explaining how things are caused" is the same as "converting them into memory stores." That is, extracting the causal history from an object is the same as viewing the object as a memory store of that history. However, the latter formulation is more powerful, since it is tied to the very concept of computation. Furthermore, I have shown that the new foundations lead to an entire re-structuring of science, in which the conventional systems of laws (e.g., Newton's laws, Einstein's field equations) are replaced by *inference rules for memory retrieval*.

For the present discussion, the crucial point is this: Whereas the conventional goal of science is to give the maximal amount of causal explanation, my new foundations give the goal of science as this: *Science is the conversion of the environment into maximal memory stores.*

4.3 New Foundations for Art

The new foundations for geometry lead to a new theory of aesthetics. By an extensive analysis of painting, music, and design, my mathematical work has shown the following:

Aesthetics is the theory of memory storage.

In fact, this proposal covers both the arts and the sciences. In the arts, I argue that the reason why art is so highly prized is this:

Artworks are maximal memory stores.

In the sciences, I argue that the reason why aesthetics is known to control much of scientific discovery is that science is the means of converting the environment into memory stores, and that aesthetics is the means of extracting the memory from those stores. In other words, both the sciences and the arts are driven to create maximal memory, and aesthetics is the means of accessing that memory. Consider, as an analogy, a computer connected to an external memory store via a cable: Aesthetics would be the means by which the computer communicated with the memory store via the cable.

Since, according to this theory, the sciences and the arts are driven by the same aim, what is the difference between them?

I argue this: Computation involves two basic operations: (1) reading a memory store, and (2) writing a memory store. The claim then becomes this: *Science* is the process of *reading* a memory store; and *art* is the process of *writing* a memory store.

Let us consider this proposal in more detail: According to the above theory, both the scientist and artist are interested in the *maximization* of memory information. The scientist focuses on maximizing the information obtained by reading. As stated in section 4.2, the scientist *converts* the environment into memory stores; in other words the scientist is interested in forcing the existing states in the environment to be memory stores. In contrast, the artist focuses on maximizing the memory information by actually creating new memory stores in the environment:

4.4 New Foundations for Computation

My new foundations for geometry are equivalent to new foundations for computation. The reason is this: In the new foundations for geometry, shape is equivalent to memory storage, and, in particular, all memory storage takes place via shape. Furthermore, the geometric theory consists of two inter-related components: (1) the inference rules for the extraction of history from shape; and (2) the generative operations which create the shape. The first of these components can be regarded as the *reading* operation in a computational process, and the second can be regarded as the *writing* operation.
These reading and writing operations are far more sophisticated than the reading and writing operations of conventional computers, where reading the state of a memory store means merely registering the state, and writing the state means merely switching it (by interchanging 0's and 1's). In contrast, in the new foundations, the reading and writing operations are, respectively, the extraction and creation of *history*, and this is based on new and very deep relations between asymmetry and symmetry, defined in our geometric theory, e.g., symmetry-breaking transfer described in Chapter 3.
Now, recall from section 4.3 that, according to the new foundations, aesthetics is the theory of memory storage. Furthermore, we said that this theory has two components: reading a memory store (which, according to the new foundations, is the function of science) and writing a memory store (which, according to the new foundations, is the function of art and design). Therefore, this claim establishes aesthetics as equivalent to computation. However, we have already said that, according to the new foundations, computation is equivalent to geometry. Therefore, this book sets up the following three-way equivalence:

GEOMETRY = COMPUTATION = AESTHETICS

Notice that the three-way equivalence exists because each of the three components is shown mathematically to be the reading and writing of memory storage.

Now, as seen above, there is a fundamental difference between the conventional theory of computation (which is the basis of contemporary computers) and the theory of computation offered in this book: the reading and writing operations that constitute the conventional theory are merely the registration and interchange of 0's and 1's; whereas in our new theory, the reading and writing operations are, respectively, the inference and generation of stored history based on symmetries and asymmetries. In fact, there is another fundamental reason why the conventional theory is different from the new theory. The conventional model of computation is that of an instruction-obeying mechanism carrying out a sequence of operations *in* time. In contrast, according to the new foundations for geometry, time is constructed from asymmetries within the present data set. That is, whereas in the conventional view, the computing system exists within time, in the new view, the computing system produces and contains time.
The production of time from asymmetries occurs as a result of converting the asymmetries into memory stores. The objects containing the asymmetries thereby become part of the computational system, i.e., become memory stores within the computational system. That is, by converting the object into a memory store, the computational system is extending itself to contain that object. Thus, according to my new foundations for geometry:

Computation is the self-creation of mind.

This contrasts with a conventional computer, which involves not only a computational process within time, but a mechanism that remains invariant through time. Opposed to this, the new theory involves not only a computational process that creates and contains time, but a mechanism that achieves this by creating *itself*. Most importantly, the system creates itself by its own reading and writing operations that act by converting and creating environmental objects as memory stores.

4.5 What is a Building?

As stated at the beginning of this chapter, the conventional view of the relationship between architecture and computation is that computers are tools in the design, manufacturing, and construc-

tion of a building. However, it was noted that this relationship is dispensable, since it uses the standard property of a computer: speed based on miniaturization of a symbolic process – a process which could be carried out by hand.
However, the above sections allow us to define an entirely new relationship between architecture and computation – one that goes to the very *function* of architecture, and is not dispensable. We saw that my new foundations for geometry are equivalent to new foundations for computation, in which the reading operation is the inference of past history from shape, and the writing operation is the generation of shape. Furthermore, whereas science is defined as the reading operation, art and design are defined as the writing operation.
Therefore, according to this theory, architecture is an example of the writing operation in a computational process. That is, according to my new foundations for architecture: *A building must act as an external hard-drive for the computational processes of a human being*.
Notice, therefore, that the relationship of a computer to architecture is not the usual one of a tool in the creation of a building. The relationship is much deeper than this: It is the person that is the computer, and the building is a hardware component that is part of this computer.
Notice the relation between this statement and the theory of time given in section 4.4: According to my new foundations for computation, time is produced by the conversion of objects into memory stores – i.e., the inference of history from shape. This contrasts with the standard theory of computation, in which the computational process takes place *in* time.
Therefore, my new foundations for computation, in which time is produced by the computational system, imply that time is produced by reading a building. In fact, since the new foundations for architecture say that a building should be a maximal memory store, the conclusion is that *a building must be an object that is a maximal source of time*.
However, the deepest aspect of the theory is this: Since the building is a memory store that extends the computational system of a person, the new foundations lead to the following principle:

A building should be an extension of the person's mind.

It is here that we have the fundamental difference between the classical foundations of architecture and the foundations proposed in this book. We have seen that, because the classical foundations are based on symmetry, they attempt to minimize memory storage in a building. In fact, when people describe the symmetrical arrangement of columns on all four sides of Palladio's Villa Rotunda as the epitome of classical perfection, I argue that they are making the following correspondence:

In the standard foundations for architecture,
perfection is equated with amnesia.

The consequence of this is that the computational processes of a human being cannot be carried out with a standard building. In other words:

A standard building is that component of the environment
that cannot be used as part of one's mind.

In contrast, my new foundations state that a building must be an object that maximally provides the capacity to be part of a person's mind; i.e., a maximal memory store. This means that a building must be an object used in the computational processes of a human being. Furthermore, these computational processes must not be the simplistic ones of a conventional computer. For, according to the new foundations, *computation is the self-creation of mind*. Most importantly, the mind creates itself by reading and writing the environment as maximal memory stores. Buildings are parts of the environment. In fact, they are the most significant parts of the environment that human beings can produce; and therefore they can be the most significant memory stores that people can actually *write*. This is what the new architecture must provide. That is:

The computational process is one in which the mind undergoes
self-creation by reading and writing itself as history.
The architectural principles, proposed in this book,
are the means by which buildings can be read and written
as the self-creation of mind. These new architectural principles
are illustrated with the administration buildings.

The Information Technology Revolution in Architecture is a new series reflecting on the effects the virtual dimension is having on architects and architecture in general. Each volume will examine a single topic, highlighting the essential aspects and exploring their relevance for the architects of today.

The IT Revolution in Architecture
edited by Antonino Saggio

Other titles in this series:

Information Architecture
Basis and Future of CAAD
Gerhard Schmitt
ISBN 3-7643-6092-5

HyperArchitecture
Spaces in the Electronic Age
Luigi Prestinenza Puglisi
ISBN 3-7643-6093-3

Digital Eisenman
An Office of the Electronic Era
Luca Galofaro
ISBN 3-7643-6094-1

Digital Stories
The Poetics of Communication
Maia Engeli
ISBN 3-7643-6175-1

Virtual Terragni
CAAD in Historical and Critical Research
Mirko Galli / Claudia Mühlhoff
ISBN 3-7643-6174-3

Natural Born CAADesigners
Young American Architects
Christian Pongratz /
Maria Rita Perbellini
ISBN 3-7643-6246-4

New Wombs
Electronic Bodies and Architectural Disorders
Maria Luisa Palumbo
ISBN 3-7643-6294-4

New Flatness
Surface Tension in Digital Architecture
Alicia Imperiale
ISBN 3-7643-6295-2

Digital Design
New Frontiers for the Objects
Paolo Martegani /
Riccardo Montenegro
ISBN 3-7643-6296-0

The Architecture of Intelligence
Derrick de Kerckhove
ISBN 3-7643-6451-3

Advanced Technologies
Building in the Computer Age
Valerio Travi
ISBN 3-7643-6450-5

Aesthetics of Total Serialism
Contemporary Research from Music to Architecture
Markus Bandur
ISBN 3-7643-6449-1

Light Architecture
New Edge City
Gianni Ranaulo
ISBN 3-7643-6564-1

Digital Gehry
Material Resistance /
Digital Construction
Bruce Lindsey

Induction Design
A Method for Evolutionary Design
Makoto Sei Watanabe
ISBN 3-7643-6641-9

The Charter of Zurich
De Kerckhove Eisenman Saggio
Furio Barzon
ISBN 3-7643-6735-0

Hyperbodies
Toward an E-motive Architecture
Kaas Oosterhuis
ISBN 3-7643-6969-8

Mathland
From Flatland to Hypersurfaces
Michele Emmer
ISBN 3-7643-0149-X

Digital Hadid
Landscapes in Motion
Michele Emmer
ISBN 3-7643-0172-4

ISBN 3-7643-6562-5
History of Form*Z
Pierluigi Serraino
ISBN 3-7643-6563-3

Flying Dutchmen
Motion in Architecture
Kari Jormakka
ISBN 3-7643-6639-7

Behind the Scenes
Avant-garde Technologies
in Contemporary Design
Francesco De Luca / Marco Nardini
ISBN 3-7643-6737-7

New Scapes
Territories of Complexity
Paola Gregory
ISBN 3-7643-6736-9

Digital Odyssey
A New Voyage in the Mediterranean
Ian+
ISBN 3-7643-6970-1

Game Zone
Playgrounds between
Virtual Scenarios and Reality
Alberto Iacovoni
ISBN 3-7643-0151-1